Drive and Stroll

North Yorkshire

Ron Freethy

COUNTRYSIDE BOOKS
NEWBURY BERKSHIRE

Cover picture of Malham Cove
supplied by David Sellman
Photographs by the author
Designed by Peter Davies, Nautilus Design

Produced through MRM Associates Ltd., Reading
Typeset by Jean Cussons Typesetting, Diss, Norfolk
Printed by Woolnough Bookbinding Ltd., Irthlingborough

Contents

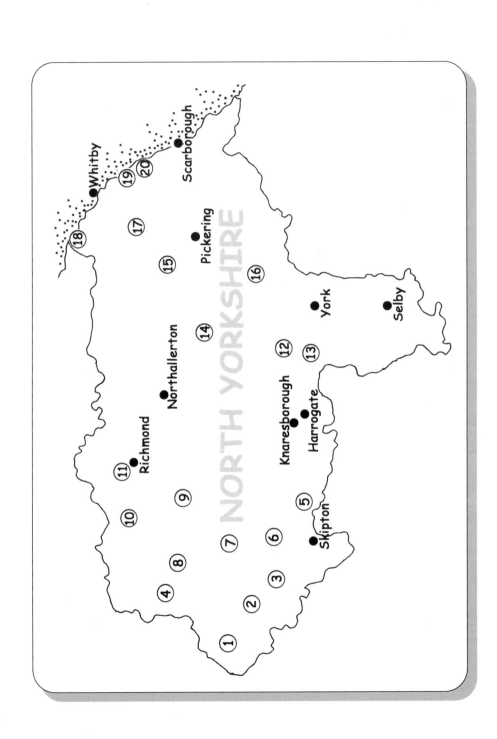

Contents ৫৵

PUBLISHER'S NOTE

We hope that you obtain considerable enjoyment from this book; great care has been taken in its preparation. Although at the time of publication all routes followed public rights of way or permitted paths, diversion orders can be made and permissions withdrawn.

We cannot, of course, be held responsible for such diversion orders and any inaccuracies in the text which result from these or any other changes to the routes nor any damage which might result from walkers trespassing on private property. We are anxious, though, that all details covering the walks are kept up to date and would therefore welcome information from readers which would be relevant to future editions.

The simple sketch maps that accompany the walks in this book are based on notes made by the author whilst checking out the routes on the ground. They are designed to show you how to reach the start, to point out the main features of the overall circuit and they contain a progression of numbers that relate to the paragraphs of the text.

However, for the benefit of a proper map, we do recommend that you purchase the relevant Ordnance Survey sheet covering your walk. The Ordnance Survey maps are widely available, especially through booksellers and local newsagents.

Introduction

North Yorkshire is one of the more impressive areas for walking in Britain. But where is it? Is it the Yorkshire Dales? – Yes. Is it the North York Moors? – Yes. Is it the East Coast? – Yes. Actually it is all of these things and more. What it is not, is an area of industrial waste.

North Yorkshire is a region of gloriously beautiful and varied countryside, with the city of York at its heart, which all agree is best explored on foot. It stretches around 100 miles from the east coast around Whitby to within less than 10 miles of the west coast near Morecambe on the Irish Sea. There is also a stretch of more than 60 miles from north to south, including coastal stretches around Whitby and Scarborough.

Kettlewell

Here then is the largest county in England and to do justice to this in the context of only 20 walks is at the very least difficult. Each walk, however, has a magnificently varied natural history and is a joy for strollers.

In the course of my work for newspapers and magazines, plus radio and television presentations, I have explored the region for almost 40 years. Whilst preparing the draft for this book I talked to three friends, the youngest of whom is 84.

'Tha'll 'ev to do like we did with our jam butties when we was kids wi no brass', he said, 'sprad it thin'. Then, with a twinkle in his eye, he added 'Don't worry lad it'll alus taste good'.

I hope that those who dip into this book don't mind it being spread thin but do find that it tastes good.

Ron Freethy

1 | Ingleton

Thornton Force

The Walk 5¾ miles ⏱3 hours
Map OS Landranger 98 (GR 695733)

How to get there

Ingleton is reached via the A65 between Settle and Kirkby Lonsdale. The village and the waterfalls walk are clearly signed off the A65. **Parking**: There is ample space at the Waterfall Trails car park (fee payable), close to the information kiosk. Please note that care should be taken to wear the correct footwear and clothing because the going can be cool and slippery.

Caution In 2004 the mapmakers still disagree regarding the naming of the rivers Twiss and Doe. OS now uses the names shown on the map given here despite the fact that Twistleton Hall and Twistleton Glen are actually on the Doe.

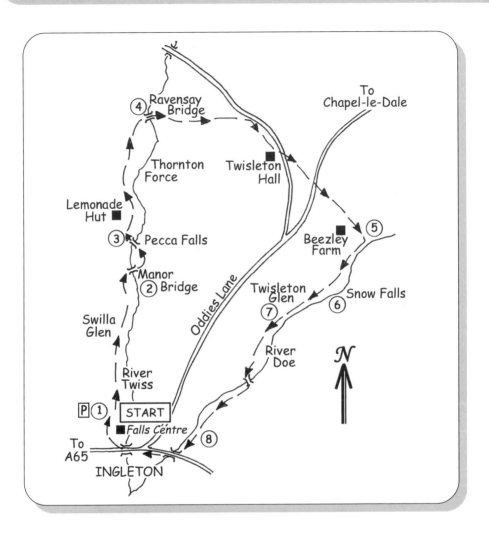

Introduction

This inspiring walk passes alongside no fewer than four major waterfalls plus a number of swirling boulder-strewn torrents. The route cuts through glens classified as SSSIs (Sites of Special Scientific Interest) and across the bed of a former lake, ground out by glacial action. It threads its way through the Craven Faults which have fascinated geologists for more than two centuries and concludes in the large village of Ingleton, which has a fascinating history.

The Wheatsheaf

This is the oldest hostelry in Ingleton, dating back to the 17th century or perhaps even earlier. It has seen service as a coaching inn and was also popular during the railway age. Ingleton was the dividing line between the Midland Railway, with its station at one end of a viaduct, and the Western Railway, with its station on the other. Travellers had to carry their bags from one station to the other and often broke their journey at the Wheatsheaf.

These days the inn provides an excellent menu for all ages and tastes from hungry walkers to families on a limited budget. Local produce is always featured prominently on the Wheatsheaf list which explains why discriminating clients visit the hostelry. Telephone 01524 241275.

THE WALK

From the **Waterfalls Trail** car park follow the track keeping the river to the right. This is always spectacular, although it is especially at its best following wet weather.

Cross through a substantial gate and enter the scenically inspiring **Swilla Glen**.

This is the place to enjoy a study of geology. There is also a magnificent display of ferns, including the common polypody, male fern, wall rue, maidenhair spleenwort, hart's tongue fern and the rare brittle bladder fern. In spring, bird life includes dipper, grey wagtail and tawny owl, whilst green and great spotted woodpecker are common. The very rare and shy lesser spotted woodpecker is also resident but more difficult to spot.

At **Manor Bridge** turn right over the river, then left towards **Pecca Falls**, this can be both seen and heard! This section follows the line of the North Craven Geological Fault and exposed areas of shale, sandstone and limestone can be seen. These rocks erode at different rates and are the reason why the waterfalls are so spectacular. Look to the left to see a 'cave' which was actually dug in the early 19th century in a fruitless search for lead.

At **Pecca Bridge** cross the river and then turn right keeping the river and the falls to the right. This area is very steep but at this point it is obvious why an entry fee to the walk is needed. Money has been well spent on the provision of splendid wooden steps and viewing areas.

Pecca Falls is a cascade of tumbling waters always interesting and, following rain or snow melt, absolutely spectacular. The steps twist and turn with new aspects of the falls appearing at every shift in

Drive and Stroll

The oldest pub in Ingleton

direction. *Over the last century writers have argued over which are the most beautiful falls – Pecca or Thornton? They are, however, so different that any comparison makes no sense.*

At the top of a steep climb go through a metal gate and pass the 'Lemonade Hut' on the left. This is a remnant of Edwardian England and still provides light refreshments when the weather seems to be suitable for a profit to be made.
Descend to **Thornton Force**.

The name 'Force' is a reminder that this was once an area settled by Scandinavians – probably the Danes. Their word for a waterfall

was force. *The views from the little picnic area are panoramic and powerful. A break here prepares for another steep climb.*

Pass up the wooden steps keeping **Thornton Force** to the right. At the top is **Raven Ray** which is the flat stony bed of what was once a glacial lake. Turn right over a bridge and follow the obvious track towards the **River Doe**.

On the right is Twistleton Hall, which is at present being restored.

Pass through **Beezley Farm** on the right and follow the track to the **River Doe**.

This is the place to watch buzzards rising on the air currents and apart from in the depths of winter there will be sightings of lapwing, curlew and skylarks which are all declining in many parts of Britain. Here common sandpiper breed in the summer but spend our cool winters in the warmth of South Africa.

 (5)

Turn right onto the riverside path and keep the river on the left to reach **Beezley Falls**.

This is another impressive area and, with no pollution in any of these streams, this is a rich area for aquatic invertebrates. Stoneflies and mayflies are abundant beneath the shelter of the stones and these insect larvae provide food for the resident dippers. Stonefly larvae have two 'tails' whilst mayfly larvae have three.

 (6)

Continue on to **Snow Falls** where the water is whipped up into a white froth, hence the name. Anyone who has seen alpine torrents in Switzerland or Norway will not be disappointed with this area.

 (7)

The route bears slightly right and then left into **Twistleton Glen**.

Here is another famous area for botanists. In spring look out for primrose, butterbur, wood sorrel, celandine, wood anemone and a host of other species. Be sure to take a flower book with you and also an extra picnic! Take your time.

 (8)

Beyond the glen a neat bridge spans the river. Cross this and turn right along the scenic path towards **Ingleton**.

Time should be spent in the village to explore the church and the Information Centre. St Mary's church is delightfully sited on a hill overlooking the rivers and stands on the site of an original Norman building with perhaps a Saxon settlement pre-dating this.

The 13th-century west tower still stands but the rest was rebuilt in 1887. Inside there is an example of what has been called a Vinegar Bible which was a translator's error – the Greek for wine was rendered as 'vinega'r! Ugh! There is also a fine Norman font with carvings showing the Slaughter of the Innocents and the Flight into Egypt.

The nearby Information Centre provides details of the village. Market day is Friday and events here show evidence of a long established farming community but there are also restored houses once occupied by the coal miners who worked in the pits of Ingleton which operated until 1937.

A short downhill stroll leads back to the **Waterfall Trails** car park.

2 Stainforth

The River Ribble at Knights Stainforth

The Walk 4 miles ⏱ 2 hours
Map OS Explorer OL 2 (GR 821673)

How to get there

From Settle just off the A65 from Long Preston go through the town centre and under the railway viaduct (Settle to Carlisle). Turn right onto the B6479. Pass the turn off for Langcliffe and find a right turn into Stainforth. **Parking**: There is a large pay and display car park in the village.

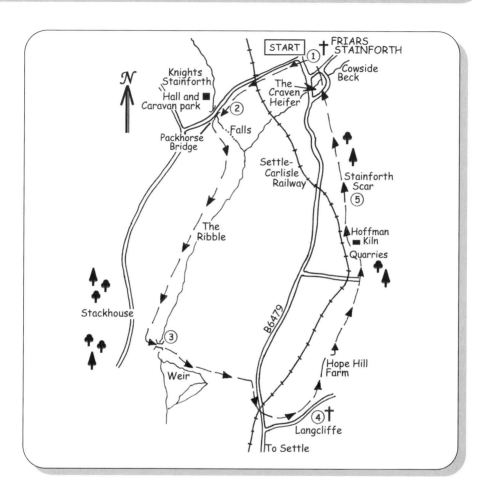

Introduction

On this walk both Stainforth and Little Stainforth can be enjoyed. They are now split by the B6479 and the Settle to Carlisle railway. The name was originally Stainford, meaning a stony ford and which is still an accurate description. The Tempest family owned Knights Stainford, now Stainforth, whilst the Cistercian monks of Sawley Abbey owned Friars Stainford, now Little Stainforth. This gentle walk passes alongside the upper reaches of the Ribble through the attractive village of Langcliffe from which can be seen magnificent limestone countryside. There is pleasure to be had not just from the sound and sight of the fast flowing Ribble but also the more gentle trickle of the tributary streams which feed it.

Drive and Stroll

The Craven Heifer

This inn offers accommodation and a varied menu. It is the place to eat steak because the heifer was indeed a formidable beast and rightly famous in this part of England. It was said to be 'substantial and prolific', which seems to be an accurate description for the hostelry at Stainforth.

The lamb and fish dishes are also excellent, the accommodation comfortable and the beer labels varied. Walkers are made welcome and so are children. Meals are served at lunchtime and in the evening from 6 pm to 9 pm. Visitors should be aware that on a few occasions during the winter the hostelry is closed on Mondays. Telephone 01729 822599.

THE WALK

(1)

Start at **Stainforth**.

Take time to stand on the stepping-stones over the beck which drains part of Malham Moor. The village is overlooked by Winskill which is a huge lump of limestone. This is surrounded by a fascinating assortment of boulders called erratics which were deposited by melting glaciers at the conclusion of the last ice age.

From the car park in the village, cross the often busy B6479, turn right and descend a narrow road to the **Ribble** in about ½ mile.

 (2)

Cross the old packhorse bridge over to **Little Stainforth** where there is a medieval hall and a caravan park.

Little Stainforth was built by the Tempest family in the 14th century but in 1547 it was bought by the

Watson family. In the 1670s Samuel Watson almost completely rebuilt the hall and also constructed the neat single arched packhorse bridge. Since 1931 the bridge has been looked after by the National Trust

At the bridge turn left through a narrow stile and follow the path close to the river which is part of the Ribble Way.

Enjoy the system of little waterfalls tumbling over huge blocks of limestone. Stainforth Force is one of the most famous beauty spots in North Yorkshire. Here there are safe places for supervised children to paddle and one or two ideal spots to picnic.

Continue along the obvious footpath towards **Langcliffe**.

Away to the right of the footpath are impressive trees and the hamlet of Stackhouse. The hall there was built around 1650 to replace an earlier Tudor hall and was the home of the

Carr family. The Carrs gave generously to the monks of Furness Abbey and in the 16th century helped in the foundation of the nearby Giggleswick School. This is lush countryside ideal for the grazing of cattle and in 1860 William Carr, who was famous for his breed of short-horned cattle including the Craven Heifer, wrote a monograph on the subject.

The beck at the start of the walk

Look out for a wooden footbridge. Cross this and continue on a path, which takes you past a weir, a reservoir and across the B6479 and the railway. Continue into **Langcliffe**.

Langcliffe is just that – it means a Long Cliff. It is one of the few villages in Upper Ribblesdale to warrant a mention in the Domesday Book. Langcliffe Hall only dates from the 19th century, although there are some parts which have been incorporated from earlier 16th and 17th century buildings. Here lived Geoffrey Dawson who was editor of The Times newspaper from 1912 to 1941.

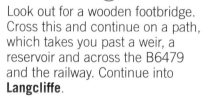

From **Langcliffe** car park, **Stainforth** is signed along a lane close to Hope Hill farm and approaches the **Hoffman Kiln**, one of the wonders of the Industrial Age. The route passes the kiln on the right, over a bridge and a stile.

The Hoffman Kiln is a huge circular brick structure of German design, consisting of many limekilns connected together in the form of a rough rectangle. These were surrounded by a railway track linking to the Settle Carlisle railway. Lime could be loaded directly into wagons and sent off to paper mills, the building industry, factories tanning leather and other industries which were working at full swing from the early 19th century.

To the right of the path leading through lush fields is **Stainforth Scar** a huge area of limestone and with lots of quarries which once provided stone for the Hoffman Kiln. Continue along a clear path and return to **Stainforth**.

Drive and Stroll

3 Kirkby Malham

The 19th-century Victoria inn

The Walk 3 miles ⏱ Allow 2 hours plus time in the church
Map OS Landranger 98 (GR 895610)

How to get there

From Skipton follow the A65 towards Gargrave. After 5 miles turn off to the right along a minor road through Bell Busk and Airton to arrive in Kirby Malham. From Settle take the B6479 for Langcliffe. Follow the road through Langcliffe to a narrow motor track to Malham. Pass Malham Tarn and Cove into Malham village. Follow signs to Gargrave to reach Kirby Malham. **Parking**: On the right is the Victoria inn, the church and free parking.

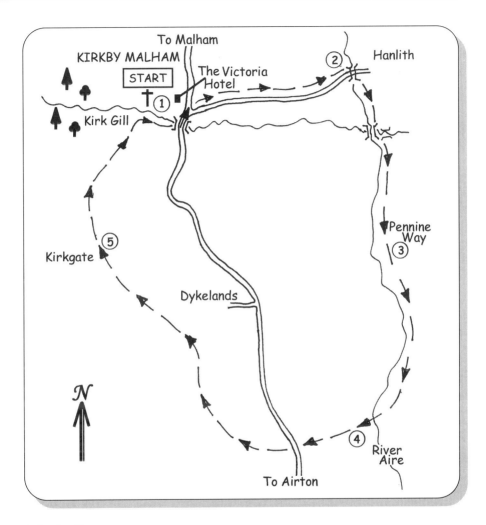

Introduction

All walkers know that Malham is one of the most spectacular areas in Britain and therefore a popular attraction. The car parks are well used and places for refreshments do a brisk trade. Kirkby Malham, where this walk is centred, is a haven of peace and tranquillity in Malhamdale. There is also an ancient church with a substantiated Oliver Cromwell connection, spectacular riverside paths and an inspiring stretch of the Pennine Way. The route is easy to walk and easy to follow, with the unpolluted headwaters of the River Aire home to fish, kingfisher, heron and in the summer the haunt of common sandpiper. Kirkby Malham has everything except a surfeit of visitors!

The Victoria

This pub was built in 1840; the menu, however, is bang up to date and includes local produce. The list of beers is also impressive. The Victoria opens daily from 12 noon and tea, coffee and sandwiches are also on offer. There are picnic tables at the front and an attractive beer garden at the rear. There is a lovely atmosphere and a sense of humour. One notice says 'Muddy Boots welcome just carry them in your hands'.
Telephone: 01729 830213.

THE WALK

Start at the **church of St Michael the Archangel**, which is the parish church for the whole area.

Kirkby Malham is at the centre of a network of villages including Otterburn, Scalegill, Airton, Calton and of course Malham itself. The latter is only about two miles from the church and was once reached by a network of riverside footpaths.

There was a church on this site from the 9th century but the present building dates from 1199 with an extensive restoration in 1879. The 70 ft (21 metres) tower was built of millstone grit in 1490. Visitors should not miss the interior with its friendly atmosphere and plentiful supply of tea, coffee and orange juice. There is a memorial to John Lambert (1619–1684) of nearby Calton who became one of Oliver Cromwell's best generals and also a close personal friend. Cromwell

attended weddings at Kirkby Malham in 1655 and he signed the visitor's book on two occasions.

Look out for a stainless steel sculpture of a kingfisher produced by local artist and blacksmith the late Bill Wild. The bird is secured to a windowsill above his favourite pew.

A sign in the churchyard leads to the Watery Grave, probably a unique edifice. Here are buried John Harrison and his wife. He was a soldier and the couple were often apart. With a sense of humour the two agreed that a little stream should separate the remains of Helen who died in 1890 and John who followed her ten years later. Thus they were separated by water in both life and death!

Approach the **Victoria** on the left, cross the road and follow the narrow cul-de-sac road which leads to **Hanlith**.

The name Hanlith means 'the hillside slope owned by the Saxon

The Watery Grave

named Hagena'. The settlement is still very small and is dominated by Hanlith Hall with a doorway carrying the name Robert Serjeantson. The presence of halberds carried on either side of the porchway show that the males of the family must have been a tough lot. A halberd is a huge and lethal combination of a battle-axe and a spear and could only be used as decoration by those who had actually used the weapon 'in a just cause'.

Cross over the **River Aire** and turn right along the **Pennine Way**.

Carry on along the Pennine Way through lush green fields and in just under 1 mile cross a bridge over the **River Aire**. This is the place to watch kingfisher, and trout can often be seen, whilst in summer common sandpipers breed.

Continue a meandering route across fields over stiles with **Dykelands** to the right and **Warber Hill Woodlands** to the left. The route is undulating but easy to follow.

The church of St Michael the Archangel

At **Kirkgate** (once a footpath route to the church) sweep gently right towards **Otterburn**. The path then forks right. Cross a footbridge over **Kirk Gill** and to return to the church and car park. You may hear the church clock. It strikes every quarter hour and provides a comforting feeling as the tuneful chimes gently interrupt the running of the **Aire** and **Kirk Beck**.

4 | Gayle and Hawes

The causeway leading to Hawes

The Walk 2¼ miles ⏱ 1½ hours
Map OS Explorer OL30 (GR 875894)

How to get there

Hawes is situated directly on the A684 west of Aysgarth. It can also be reached from Junction 37 of the M6 and the B6255 via Ingleton. Approaching from the B6255, Gayle is signed to the right. There are no refreshments in Gayle apart from at the Creamery but this does not matter because it helps to create the atmosphere of an old village.
Parking: There is a small pay and display car park in the village, plus some street parking.

Drive and Stroll

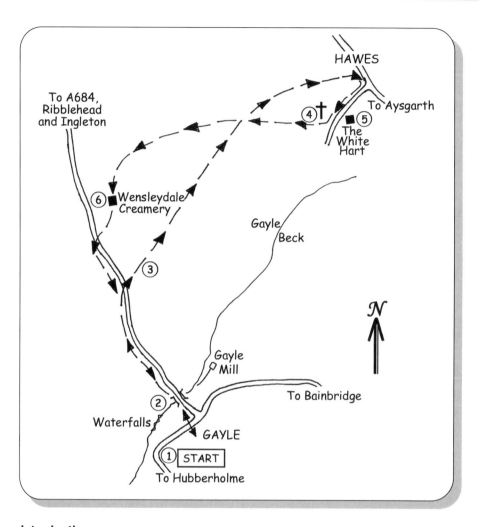

To A684, Ribblehead and Ingleton

HAWES

To Aysgarth

④ †

⑤ The White Hart

⑥ ■ Wensleydale Creamery

Gayle Beck

③

N

Gayle Mill

To Bainbridge

② Waterfalls

GAYLE

① START

To Hubberholme

Introduction

Gayle is one of those underrated areas which has altered little since the mid 19th century. The route includes wonderful sights and sounds as Gayle Beck drains part of Langstrothdale and rushes down to meet the River Ure. The area around Gayle and Hawes was once known as Yoredale or Uredale until its name was changed to Wensleydale. Until the 16th century the monks of Furness, Fountains and Jervaulx reared horses and sheep on the slopes of the Ure. They made cheese from sheep's milk and the Wensleydale Creamery, passed on this gentle stroll, uses the modified methods of production perfected by the monks, although cows' milk is now used. This is a walk of contrasts with the old-time tranquillity of Gayle blending well with the hustle and bustle of Hawes.

The White Hart in Hawes

There is no shortage of hostelries in Hawes but my favourite is the White Hart. From the outside it looks like a typical town pub but once inside its character comes alive whilst its menu is mouth-watering. There is anything from morning tea or coffee, soup and a sandwich to Yorkshire gammon, Whitby scampi, local beef and lamb and, of course, a wide choice of cheeses, many of which are local. Telephone: 01969 667259.

THE WALK

Start in the centre of **Gayle** and look at old cottages on the right and the old ford on the beck to the left. This is still used by local traffic and in dry weather brave souls use the improvised stepping-stones to cross. Continue onwards keeping the beck to the left.

Turn left and stop by the bridge to view the tumbling cascades of small waterfalls upstream, which look at their best when rain is followed by sunshine. Look out for the resident dipper and grey wagtail.

Downstream and to the right is Gayle Mill, which made the headlines in the summer of 2004 by becoming the regional finalist in the BBC's series, Restoration. *From 2005 onwards the Friends of Gayle Mill will be busy ensuring that the*

18th-century water-powered cotton mill and the later timber mill will be preserved. It will eventually become a major tourist attraction because it was one of the first such mills to be built in Britain.

From the bridge pass down the main street for a short distance before finding a footpath sign on the right. Pass through two metal gates, which lead onto a substantial stone causeway through fields. There are magnificent views down to **Gayle Beck** and the Mill. Continue along the track.

Approach **Hawes** church through stiles but keep the church to the right. The name Hawes is derived from *hawse* which is Old Norse and means a mountain pass. Looking towards the church this description is very accurate. Follow a narrow causeway which descends through a complex of cottages and then underneath one of them. This alley

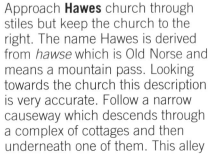

Drive and Stroll

Gayle

leads down into the busy main street.

Turn right and if there is time visit the **Countryside Centre and Museum** which is housed in the disused railway station. There is also a Rope Works on the same site.

 ⑤

The road forks left to the Rope Works and right to the **White Hart** which is on the left of the road. Opposite the pub is a very small sign on the wall which indicates Gayle Lane. Ascend the lane and pass the church on the right. At a complex of stiles go straight ahead through the cemetery to the right. A gap leads to the car park of the **Wensleydale Creamery**. Here is a museum of cheese making, a viewing gallery where modern production methods can be seen, a café and a shop obviously selling cheese but also souvenirs.

 ⑥

The exit to the creamery meets the minor road between **Gayle** and **Hawes**. Turn left and return to the starting point which is less than ½ mile.

5 Bolton Abbey

The Walk 4 miles 🕐 Allow at least 3 hours and longer if you want to explore the Abbey. (Entrance free but there is a parking fee for those who do not arrive on foot).
Map OS Landranger 104 (GR 026533)

How to get there

From Skipton follow the A59 towards York and Harrogate. Bolton Abbey Steam Railway Station is signed to the right. **Parking**: There is plenty of free parking at the station. Some stretches of the walk can be muddy after wet weather so suitable footwear should be worn.

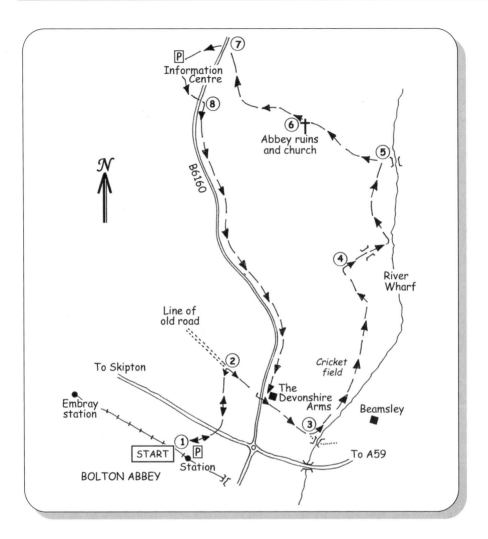

Introduction

Our stroll follows glorious countryside, babbling little brooks and the sweeping meander of the River Wharfe. This enfolds one of the most majestic religious houses in Britain, Bolton Abbey. The village of Embsay and Bolton Abbey have a connection because the Augustinian monks built their first abbey at Embsay. By 1154, however, they found the windy upland site to be too demanding and the brethren removed to a more peaceful site at Bolton on the banks of the Wharfe.

This route is not just a drive and stroll but has the added bonus of being a steam and stroll thanks to the Embsay and Bolton Abbey Railway if you so wish. The presence of the short steam journey is a pleasant reminder of travel in a more leisurely age. The return trip to Embsay takes around an hour. In the village is a pleasant craft shop housed in an old mill.

Station Buffet, Bolton Abbey

At the station is this splendid little café and on cooler days the coal fire is warm and welcoming. The food is best described as basic but excellent, much of it being literally home-made by volunteers. Down the rail line is Embsay station with its own pleasant little teashop. Telephone: 0176 710614.

THE WALK

From the car park, walk away from the station. Before reaching the old railway bridge find a footpath to the left. Turn left. The bridge was once part of the rail extension long since closed. Pass through a gate and see the A59 road in the distance. Descend through a field. Cross over a, usually dry, streambed and then between walls and a little bridge over a pretty stream. Bear sharp right.

Keep the stream to the right and pass beneath an ugly but nevertheless functional bridge carrying the busy A59 over the tributaries of the **Wharfe**. Turn sharp left, and ascend a path towards a substantial fence.

At the fence pass through a gate and turn right. This is now a footpath and bridleway but until the new A59 was built it was the narrow and winding main road. Approach a substantial gate from which there are magnificent views of fields to the right and meadows overlooked by rolling hills to the left.

Come up to the **Devonshire Arms Country House Hotel**, which has been owned by the dukes of Devonshire since 1773. Meals and snacks are on offer and there is a pleasant open-air area well used in the summer. Pass through the gate and cross the B6160, which is on the bus routes 72 and 74 which link to Skipton and Ilkley.

Turn right past the Devonshire Arms and to the right are the **Abbey Tea Rooms** where there is also a substantial car park. In a short distance turn left along a track marked **Beamsley Lane**.

This leads to the old Bolton Bridge which has spanned the River Wharfe since the Middle Ages.

Drive and Stroll

Footbridge over the River Wharfe

At one time the bridge carried traffic but this has now been closed leaving the structure safe from vibrations and in splendid isolation.

 (3)

At the bridge look for footpath sign indicating **Bolton Abbey**. Turn left. Keep the **Wharfe** on the right and Bolton Abbey cricket field and the Devonshire Arms on the left.

Look up to the right and above the river see the hamlet of Beamsley, which has a set of Lady Anne

Clifford almshouses dating to the mid 17th century. Now owned by the Landmark Trust, the almshouses can be hired by the week.

 (4)

Cross a stile and at this point the abbey is clearly seen.

On the riverbank is a fenced-off area designed to conserve the natural vegetation along the riverbank. Anglers are often to be seen beyond this area. Permits to fish can be obtained from the Bolton Abbey Estates Office.

Continue along the track, which gently sweeps first left and then right until it is close to the bank of the **Wharfe**.

This area has lots of quiet nooks and crannies full of flowers and viewing areas which birds, and therefore bird watchers, love.

Continue to bear right, crossing a small wooden bridge. This does not cross the river but spans the damp areas of the old monastic fish ponds. There were also drainage channels feeding into the **Wharfe**.

Approach a substantial wooden footbridge over the **Wharfe** but do not cross it. This and the nearby stepping-stones, which preceded the bridge, are popular with visitors and on warm days a van sells locally made ice cream.

Turn left, away from the **River Wharfe**, and follow a track keeping the river on the right. Ascend the path through a stile before climbing the stone steps to **Bolton Abbey** ruins and church. These should be explored at leisure, especially the cloister area where the monks themselves used to rest

The Priory Church of St Mary and St Cuthbert is a joy and is still in use. Enter slowly (visitors are always welcome whatever they are wearing) and allow the soothing music to take over.

Bolton's church survived when Henry VIII dissolved the rest of the monastery in 1539. The Augustinians were not 'normal' monks who thrived on isolation but they were priests who allowed the local people to worship with them. Bolton survived because it was the parish church of local folk although the rest of the abbey was dissolved. This was another name for being demolished for its valuable timber and lead roofing.

From the church climb the gentle slope up to Bolton Abbey village taking care when meeting the often busy B6160.

Turn left and follow the roadside footpath downhill all the way back to the Devonshire Arms. Look for the Old Road Bridlepath. Turn right and then left through the gate. Retrace the route back to the station car park

6 Linton-in-Craven

Linton

The Walk 4 miles ⏱ 2½ hours
Map OS Landranger 98 (GR 002627)

How to get there

From the A59 road between Skipton and Bolton Abbey look for a roundabout. Take the left exit onto the B6265 which is signed Grassington. Continue for about 6 miles before passing a large limestone quarry on the left. Just beyond this find a right turn signed to Linton. **Parking**: On all but the busiest of days there is sufficient free parking in the village close to the Fountaine Inn.

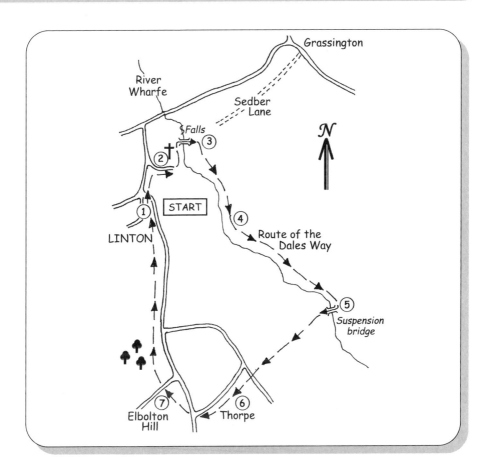

Introduction

This walk has everything – an old pub, a set of historic almshouses, packhorse bridges, river crossings, waterfalls and weirs, riverside scenery and two pretty and historic villages. Old cottages and an even older church are sure to delight as are the remains of watermills once powered by the River Wharfe as it surges through limestone gorges. The wildlife is spectacular on every day of the year.

The Fountaine Inn

This hostelry dates to the 17th century and still retains its old world charm, with small rooms and intimate nooks and crannies. The menu, however, is

modern but also includes local produce and traditional dishes. A variety of beers, again including some brewed locally, are on offer, and tea and coffee are always available during trading hours. Walkers are welcome. All that is asked is for visitors to wipe their boots at the door.
Telephone: 01756 752210.

THE WALK

###

Start at **Linton** green.

Look at an impressive obelisk, which bears an inscription: 'A tribute to Linton-in-Craven on being adjudged first in the News Chronicle loveliest village in the North West Contest in 1949.'
The village is still a delight, the memorial remains in fine fettle but the News Chronicle *has long faded into history. On the opposite side of the green is an attractive set of almshouses and its associated chapel known as Fountaine's hospital. These were set up by Richard Fountaine in 1721. He was a local lad who became a timber merchant in London and made a huge fortune from the reconstruction of the city following the Great Fire of 1666.*

At the chapel turn left over an ancient clapper bridge and then left again. Pass the 14th-century packhorse bridge on the left and approach the present road bridge dating to 1890. Turn right along the road. At a crossroads carry straight on following the signs for **Linton** church and Falls. Descend to the church where there is another car park (Pay and Display).

###

Follow straight ahead past lovely old cottages to the **Church of All Saints**, which serves not just Linton but also Grassington and Threshfield.

The church has Norman origins but it is accepted that there was a place of Christian worship on the banks of the Wharfe as early as the 5th century. The pagan religions always attached great significance to meanders of rivers and the Christians simply took over the pagan site. Look for the bosses on the church, which shows a green man with his head wreathed in vegetation. Perhaps early Christians did not reject all their pagan beliefs based on the natural world completely!

From the church retrace the route past the car park alongside the road lined with old cottages and a number of watermills now converted into dwellings. Turn right through a group of buildings to **Linton Falls**.

Linton Falls and footbridge are a joy for those who like spectacular

The old mill workings, Linton

scenery and industrial archaeology. Some of the watermills have been converted into dwellings, although two remain, albeit almost in ruins and with much of their machinery intact but rusting. Here is an irresistible combination of natural limestone gorges and man-made weirs.

 (3)

Turn right across a footbridge and then sharp right to follow part of the **Dales Way** running alongside the river.

The Dales Way is an 81-mile (130 km) waymarked track which links Ilkley with Bowness-on-Windermere. This little section is delightfully easy to follow and is much favoured by naturalists who love the flowers in the summer months whilst birdwatchers often prefer the winter when the resident dippers, kingfishers and grey wagtails are joined by wildfowl such as goosander and goldeneye.

 (4)

Continue straight ahead and reach a substantial suspension bridge, which links **Hebden** on the left bank with **Thorpe** on the right.

The bridge, which has been restored in recent years, dates to 1885 and was built by William Bell who was the Hebden blacksmith.

Cross the bridge and turn left to find a sign to the right indicating the steep path to **Thorpe**. At the top of the hill pause for breath, bear right and descend into **Thorpe**.

Thorpe has a triangular-shaped green dominated by a maypole and no dwelling is more attractive than the old Manor House dating to the 16th century.

The Fountaine Inn, Linton

From Thorpe village green find an obvious path which sweeps to the right. Ascend this track to meet a T-junction. Turn left and after almost a mile find a stone step stile.

Don't rush this section but enjoy the views of Elbolton Hills. This is actually an ancient reef knoll and dates back to carboniferous times (345 million years ago). At this time the area was a shallow tropical sea and eventually this evaporated to produce ridges of limestone reefs, which are full of fossils. These are all that remain of shelled organisms which once dominated the sea. Many reef knolls have been quarried for concrete and other chemicals. Elbolton is one of the most beautifully preserved coral reefs in the county.

From a stile a path leads through deciduous woodland rich in wildlife especially flowers typical of limestone. Look out for dog rose, bird's foot trefoil, kidney vetch and a host of other species. The track is easy to follow and once through the wood, look for a ladder stile. Climb this and return to **Linton** village.

7 Kettlewell

The tea room in Kettlewell

The Walk 4½ miles ⏱2½ hours
Map OS Landranger 98 (GR 969724)

How to get there

From Skipton on the A59 turn off along the B6265 signed 'Grassington'. Then follow the B6160 through Kilnsey to Kettlewell. **Parking**: Turn right into the village, cross a bridge over the River Wharfe and, almost immediately left is a pay and display car park.

Drive and Stroll

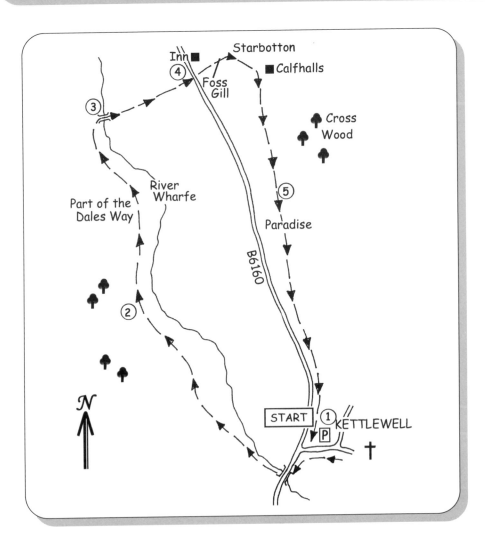

Introduction

Kettlewell has Anglo-Saxon origins and was called *cetel wella* which translates as 'a bubbling stream'. This can be appreciated all along this easy to follow stroll as can the ancient method of terracing fields which were called lynchets. A 4,000-year-old skeleton was found near the village in 1997 and there are also clear signs of the presence of the Brigantes tribes in Iron Age times, as well as evidence of later Roman occupation. None of these people disturbed the tranquillity of Upper Wharfedale and neither did the lead mining industry or the days of the stagecoach when there were no fewer than thirteen alehouses. Today, only three of these inns remain. These are the Bluebell, which dates to 1680, and the Racehorses which is actually wrongly named. It should really be Rash Horses. At one time this hostelry was the stable block for the Blue Bell and the horses here were used to help heavy coaches up the steep incline at Park Rash.

The third hostelry is the 17th-century Kings Head, which at one time was used as the local workhouse. The circular walk has history and natural history in abundance and the hamlet of Starbotton has attractive 17th-century cottages and the Fox and Hounds Inn, which was rebuilt following a flood in the 19th century.

The Cottage Tea Room

Unusually for a tea room, it offers 'Four Poster Bed and Breakfast' but for casual visitors there is also a varied menu including Yorkshire roast ham and succulent casseroles, often incorporating local meats. There is also a wide choice for vegetarians. Forget your diet and sample the wide selection of home-made sweets with seasonal local fruits often in evidence. Telephone: 01756 792605.

THE WALK

Kettlewell village is popular throughout the year with its maypole and quaint cottages. A trickling stream splits the village in two on its way to join the Wharfe. It seems strange to discover that in the 19th century Kettlewell had a water-powered cotton mill proving that Lancashire did not have a monopoly. In the days of lead and cotton the village was full of hustle and bustle. To sample the atmosphere of these days visit in late August when the Scarecrow Festival is in full swing, sure proof that Kettlewell is still a farming community.

From the car park retrace your steps and cross the bridge over the **Wharfe** and turn sharp right. Follow the riverside footpath which is along the **Dales Way** long distance footpath. The signs indicate **Buckden** with **Starbotton** along the way.

Pass through stiles and kissing gates but at all times the grassy footpath is obvious.

Between two belts of woodland it is a joy for those who love wildlife. In the trees are great spotted woodpecker, jay and sparrowhawk. There are plenty of places to picnic

Drive and Stroll

On the route at Starbotton

and so this is a delightful stroll for those with children. This whole area is dog friendly but there are sheep in some of the fields so a lead is essential.

  (3)

Approach a substantial wooden footbridge over the **Wharfe**.

A plaque on this span carries a dedication to the memory of Harry Smith who was the former chairman of the West Riding Ramblers.

At the bridge there is a signpost indicating **Arncliffe** to the left, with **Buckden** straight ahead. Turn right over the footbridge and follow the grassy track towards **Starbotton**. One track leads off to the left. Ignore this and carry straight on.

  (4)

Approach a gate leading onto the B6160 connecting **Kettlewell** and **Starbotton**. Cross the B6160. To the left is Starbotton hamlet and the quaint little **Fox and Hounds pub** well worth a diversion of only 100 yards (30 metres) but our route follows a track to find **Foss Gill House**. Turn right over a stile at Foss Gill. A finger signpost indicates 'Kettlewell 2

The Scarecrow Festival

miles'. Pass through a metal gate and the path climbs gently through fields to a gap in a wall to an old barn called **Calfhalls**. Follow through a field stile and over a set of steps.

On the left is Cross Wood, another wonderful place for naturalists and down to the right is the valley of the Wharfe carved out by glaciers at the conclusion of the last Ice Age around 10,000 years ago. Overlooking the valley are limestone hills proving that prior to the ice the area was much warmer and covered by a shallow sea. Climate variations are nothing new to Mother Nature.

Continue across undulating fields and stone stiles through an area very appropriately called Paradise. Pass farm buildings on the right over a series of simple stiles and return to **Kettlewell**.

8 | Bainbridge and Semerwater

Tranquil Semerwater

The Walk 6 miles ⏰ 3 hours
Map OS Landranger 98 (GR 935903)

How to get there

Bainbridge is set on the A684 linking Hawes and Aysgarth. From Skipton the B6160 leads through Kettlewell, Starbotton and Buckden through Bishopsdale to Aysgarth. A left turn along the A684 leads to Bainbridge.
Parking: There is parking along the extensive village green. There is also a pay car park on the shores of Semerwater: Tickets for the car park can be obtained from a farm near the fishing club.

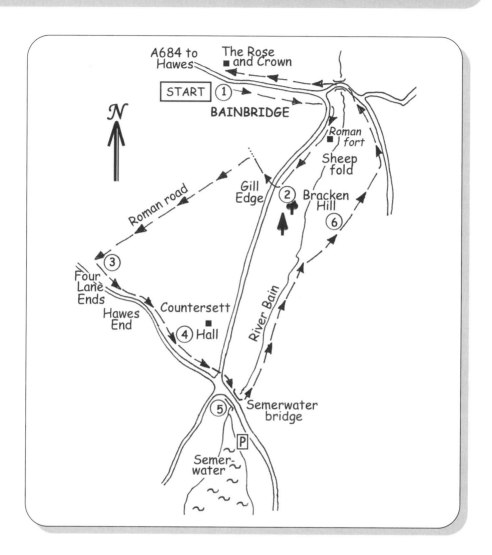

Introduction

This walk is quite strenuous but well worth the effort as it follows the line of a Roman road, crosses what is said to be the shortest river in England and passes the shoreline of Semerwater, one of only two natural lakes in Yorkshire. In the Middle Ages the whole of this area was forested and throughout this circuit there is still some evidence of this ancient woodland.

Drive and Stroll

The Rose and Crown

There can be very few hostelries with such a fascinating history as the Rose and Crown, which dates back to 1445. From the Feast of the Holy Rood (September 27th) to Shrovetide in the spring, a villager, usually one of the Metcalf family, who once were lords of nearby Nappa Hall, stands on the steps of the inn and blows an ancient horn. The sound is said to travel for three miles and at dusk it once guided travellers through the woodlands to the safety of the inn. The Rose and Crown is a large hostelry with lots of attractive nooks and crannies and a menu which reflects both local and international tastes. Telephone: 01969 650225.

THE WALK

Start at the village green overlooked by the **Rose and Crown** and on which stands a splendid set of stocks.

The village is actually owned by the residents, which has been the case since the reign of Charles II. At that time the locals purchased the manorial rights of Bainbridge from the City of London. Look out also for the attractive cottages and other buildings including the Dame's School which in the 1860s was run by a formidable lady called Mrs Eliza Blades.

Head towards the A684 before turning right towards **Gill Edge**.

At **Gill Edge** turn right and then left to follow a Roman road.

There is a raised area above Bainbridge which is the site of a Roman fort. From this an almost ruler straight road leads off to Ribchester on the banks of the Ribble in Lancashire a distance of around 36 miles. The Roman name for Bainbridge was Virosidium. There is one great advantage in following Roman roads – they are usually so straight that it is impossible to get lost. The Romans were present in this area from AD 80 until around AD 380.

The Roman road turns left to Hawes End.

The track leads into the settlement of **Countersett** reached by a descent, through stiles and close to stone walls.

Countersett is set in remote countryside and was thus in an ideal area for the Quakers to establish a firm base. Look out for Countersett Hall which was visited by George Fox in 1677. It was the home of Richard Robinson who died in 1693 but not before he had

The Carlow Stone

established a Quaker burial ground in Bainbridge. Notice also the refurbished Friends Meeting House in the hamlet.

  (4)

From Countersett descend sharply and bear first right and then left to Semerwater Bridge at which point the Bain flows out of the lake.

Take time to enjoy the sights and sounds of Semerwater. Look out for the huge Carlow Stone made of limestone and which was carried by a retreating glacier. In the Bronze Age there is said to have been a village here with dwellings set on stilts.

In summer Semerwater is enjoyed by boaters and water skiers but in winter these activities are curtailed to allow wintering wildfowl the solitude they need.

The monks of Jervaulx had a grange (farm) on the banks of Semerwater but they shared this area with the lords of Middleham Castle who had a hunting lodge on the bank.

From **Semerwater Bridge** follow the river, keeping the watercourse on the left. The path climbs steadily and passes through a number of well-maintained stiles. **Bracken Hill** is at the summit of the walk and the views from it through the mixed stretch of woodland are impressive.

A steep descent leads to a gate and a stile close to which is a large sheepfold.

These folds were essential during the Middle Ages and until well into the 19th century. Each shepherd marked his sheep by 'lug clips', which were shapes clipped in the ears, and strays were gathered in the sheepfold. A shepherd's meet in these places ensured that man and sheep were eventually reunited.

From the sheepfold follow the footpath and reach a minor road on the right. Turn left and then left again across the substantial bridge over the **Bain**.

Spend some time enjoying the views from the bridge over the Bain which are equally impressive both downstream and upstream. The

The River Bain

Bain flows out of Semerwater and runs for only 2 miles to its confluence with the Ure just beyond Bainbridge. Its course of only 2 miles earns it the title of England's shortest river. What it makes up for in length is more than compensated for by its beauty.

Return to **Bainbridge** (called Brough in Roman times), dominated here by the elevated site of the old Roman fort. This controlled the area of modern-day Wensleydale and was important farmland for the Romans.

9 Middleham

Middleham Castle

The Walk 3½ miles 🕐 2 hours
Map OS Explorer OL 30 (GR 125876)

How to get there

Middleham is signed off the A684, which links Wensley to Leyburn. From Wensley a minor road links to the A6108. Turn right from this into Middleham. **Parking**: Even on busy days there seems to be free parking on the streets and on the cobbled square.

Drive and Stroll

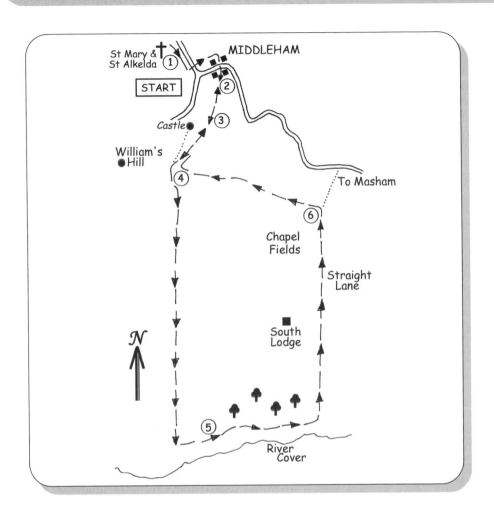

Introduction

Middleham was a stronghold of Richard III and, despite Shakespeare's condemnation of him, he was much loved in this area. The little town, said to be the smallest in England, is full to bursting with horses because there are many racing stables located in the centre. This walk passes stables containing fine breeds of horses, two castles and lush grassy paths along the banks of the River Cover, one of the major tributaries of the River Ure.

The skill of the horse breeder dates back to the days of the monks who lived nearby at Jervaulx. Richard III would have been aware of this and many of his steeds would have been Middleham bred.

The Nosebag teashop and Richard III pub

The route of this walk passes an excellent tea shop and an attractive pub. The two share picnic tables where diners can enjoy the almost constant sight and sound of horses on their way to and from the gallops.

The Nosebag serves delicious snacks including home-made sweets but is only open from Thursday to Sunday. Telephone: 01969 625558. The **Richard III** pub is also a welcoming spot with lots of local produce on the menu. In the evening it is often full of racing folk and, who knows, you may be able to pick up a tip or two. Telephone: 01969 623240.

THE WALK

(1)

Start from the grounds of the church of **St Mary and St Alkelda**.

The latter was a Saxon princess who was killed by pagan Danish women because of her Christian faith. A Norman church was built here from a Saxon base. Richard of Gloucester set up a collegiate church here in 1478 designed for the training of priests. Richard was much loved in Middleham and was not a hunchback. He had one arm slightly longer than the other but was an athlete and a skilful fighter. Richard probably did have the Princes killed in the Tower but in the context of the period he was no worse than Henry VIII, Bloody Mary or even Elizabeth the Virgin Queen herself.

From the church cross the A6108, ascend the road and find the town square on the left.

(2)

From the square look for the

Nosebag cafe and the **Richard III pub**. Between the two find a narrow alleyway and walk through it.

(3)

On meeting a wider track turn right and continue on to the substantial castle ruins. Pass the castle and its now dry moat on the right.

The castle is in the care of English Heritage and there is an entry fee. It is open daily in season but in the winter months it is closed on Mondays. Richard of Gloucester was trained here as a knight from the age of eleven and at nineteen married his childhood sweetheart Ann Neville but his life was short as he was killed at the age of 32. His only son Prince Edward died in infancy and so the Plantagenet line died out.

(4)

At a metal gate look to the right where horses can be seen grazing. Look for an earthworks to the right.

This is William's Hill where there was an earlier effort by the Normans

The Nosebag is passed on the walk

to build a castle. This was almost certainly on the site of an Iron Age fort. The original motte and bailey protected the approaches to Wensleydale and Coverdale but was abandoned in 1170 when the new castle was constructed.

Follow an uphill path, with a stout wall on the right, before descending across fields to the **River Cover**.

 (5)

At the river, turn left and continue parallel with its banks, keeping the woodlands to the left. There is quite a steep climb around the woods and in wet weather it can be slippery. It looks a joy when snow is on the ground and providing the right clothing is worn there is no problem. The path diverges at times but <u>always</u> proceed to the right along a track which follows the bank of the river.

The obvious path now emerges from the woodland, through a stile and then turns left onto a track. This continues ahead and passes **South Lodge** on the left.

 (6)

At **Chapel Fields**, the footpath sweeps to the left. Follow this track keeping a wall to the right. Continue on this path until you return to point (4) with William's Hill over to the left. Turn right here and return to the castle, now on the left and retrace your steps to the starting point.

10 | Reeth and Grinton

The path through St Andrew's churchyard

The Walk 5 miles ⏱ 2½ hours
Map OS Landranger 98 (GR 040988)

How to get there

Set on the old coach road linking Richmond and Lancaster, the best route today is via the A6108 from Richmond and turning off right onto the B6270 to Reeth. It can also be reached from Leyburn and from Aysgarth off the A684. **Parking**: There is plenty of parking on payment of a small fee on Reeth Green but this can be limited on Fridays when there is a street market.

Drive and Stroll

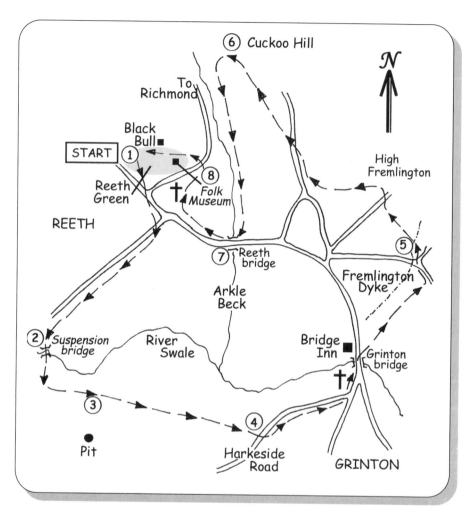

Introduction

Over a century ago Reeth and the district around it was a hive of industry, with lead mining and smelting belching acrid smoke. Now the area of Swaledale is walking country, its river and feeder streams unpolluted and abounding with wildlife. This route takes in one of the most substantial parish churches to be found in Northern England. The history of the whole area is explained by exhibits within the Swaledale Folk Museum. After closing during 2004 for a major refurbishment it opened again in 2005 and is situated just off the main square in Reeth.

The Black Bull Hotel

This is one of many old coaching inns set around the centre of Reeth, proving just what an important stop this was. It prides itself on being a 'traditional Yorkshire pub' with real ale and real Yorkshire grub. There are thick soups, steak and kidney pies and puddings and its Sunday carvery is as good as anywhere in the land. The open fires are locally famous. Telephone: 01748 884213.

THE WALK

From the street opposite the **Black Bull** find a sign indicating the river. Do not cross the river at this point but turn right and follow a narrow lane. Descend to a gate and bear slightly right. Then turn left to the river.

Cross the river over what is known as the suspension bridge and which demonstrates the power of the fast-flowing **Swale**, which has long been prone to flooding. The bridge was built in 1933 but was swept away by a storm in the floods of 2000. Rebuilding has been a problem but there is still a crossing. Turn left keeping the Swale on the left.

Keep a look out for the old fields showing Anglo-Saxon cultivation terraces known as lynchets. These are best seen when outlined by the winter frosts. Look to the right for an area known as a disused 'pit'. This is not lead or coal but marl which was a rich mix of lime and clay and,

until the advent of modern fertilisers, an essential mixture for farmers.

Continue to follow the line of the Swale until **Harkeside Road** is reached. Turn left.

Continue to the **church of St Andrew**.

This substantial structure is known as the Cathedral of the Dales. For centuries this was the only parish church in Upper Swaledale and parts date from the 12th century but most of the church was constructed between the 14th and 16th centuries. The church is usually open in daylight hours and the interior is impressive. Take care not to touch some of the gravestones which are in an unstable condition. The church has a hagioscope best known as a Lepers Squint. This allowed infected people to watch the church service without going inside and contaminating the healthy. The church began life as a mission church established by the Augustinian Canons of Bridlington Priory.

Drive and Stroll

Cross **Grinton Bridge** and follow the road for a short distance. Close to the **Bridge Inn** turn right along a footpath. Cross stiles on a footpath to **High Fremlington**. Look out for **Fremlington Dyke** built by the Brigantes tribe as a defence against the Romans.

A 'traditional' Yorkshire pub

 (5)

Follow minor roads first left and then right. A footpath signposted Fremlington leads through fields. High Fremlington is traditional sheep country and this is the place to see the Swaledale breed and the collies which work them so well.

Turn right and follow a signpost to **Arkengarthdale**. Ascend this path as it climbs towards **Cuckoo Hill**.

 (6)

From Cuckoo Hill the easy-to-follow path sweeps left and offers splendid views of Reeth whilst to the right is the substantial tributary of Arkle Beck, which tumbles its way down to meet the Swale. Descend through fields to **Reeth Bridge** itself

damaged by floods although parts of the span remain and date to the early 18th century.

 (2)

Cross Reeth Bridge and turn right. Then bear right to the recently refurbished **Swaledale Folk Museum** which is open from Good Friday until the end of October .

Life in Swaledale was to say the least varied and there are displays from dry stone walling through to butter making. The knitting of stockings was a local craft with a pair donated to Elizabeth I and in the 18th century as many as 1,800 pairs were exported each year. The main export now is tourism and this is delivered with the same Swaledale efficiency.

11 | Richmond and Easby Abbey

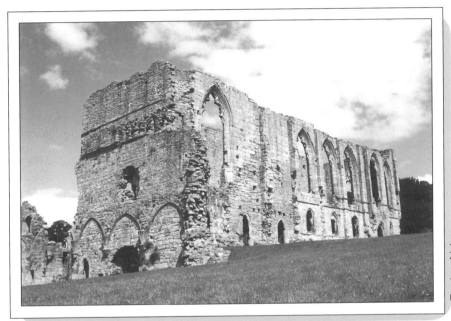

Easby Abbey

The Walk 3½ miles ⏱ 2 hours
Map OS Landranger 92 (GR 168012)

How to get there

Richmond is close to the A1 and can be reached from Catterick Bridge or from Scotch Corner via the A6108. From Leyburn, Richmond is reached via the A6108 with turn offs into Swaledale. **Parking**: As befits an ancient market town, Richmond has lots of pay and display car parks but there is also some disc parking. On busy Saturdays, parking can be a problem but at all other times, there is parking in and around the market square near the castle. There is also free parking by the old railway station.

Drive and Stroll

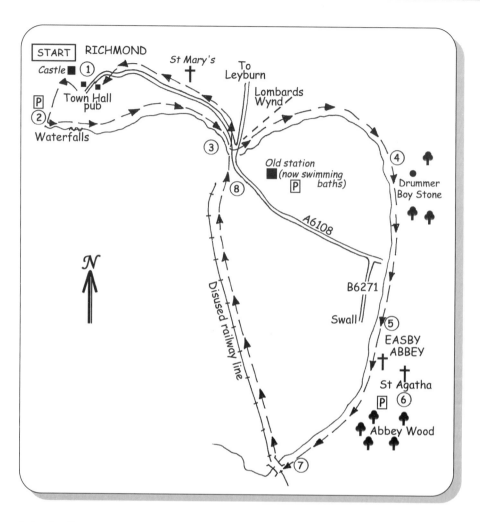

Introduction

This walk has everything including a spectacular castle, sparkling waterfalls and riverside paths, plus a disused railway line connecting the town to the ancient abbey at Easby. Add to this the occasional sighting of kingfishers along the Swale and stretches of ancient woodland which must have been enjoyed by the monks at Easby. Historians, natural historians or a family in search of a pleasant picnic will all be delighted with this gentle stroll. There are numerous hostelries in Richmond especially around the market square. Find the obelisk which dates to 1771 and replaced the ancient market cross. Beneath this is the old well, which provided drinking water probably since Saxon times. Modern drinkers will enjoy the atmosphere of the Old Town Hall pub. Opposite this is my choice of food stop.

Barber's

This is one of the best fish and chip shops in the whole of Yorkshire and that is saying something. There is a take-away but upstairs is an excellent air-conditioned restaurant. It offers a varied menu, ideal for families, with an amazing variety of species of fish to go with 'home-made' chips.

THE WALK

Between the **Town Hall pub** opposite **Barber's** and the old covered market, turn right along a narrow road. The entrance to the castle is reached within a few yards.

This huge edifice looms over Swaledale and was completed by 1180. The views from the curtain walls are spectacular and well worth the admission fee. The ruins are well cared for by English Heritage.

Facing the castle turn left and then right and descend an alley known as a wynd. This is an old English word meaning a spiral and constructed to connect two streets.

Descend stone steps and turn left by the waterfalls along the Swale. Here is a car park and a snack bar serving ice cream. Alongside the spectacular falls is a picnic site. From the picnic site follow the riverside footpath and on through a grassy parkland overlooked by a school. The route veers to the left.

A metal gate leads to the main road; cross this and turn left onto a track. Ensure that the River Swale is on the right. Pass through **Lombard's Wynd**, with a view of the parish church of St Mary the Virgin up to the left.

Inside the church there are some impressive choir stalls salvaged from Easby Abbey following its dissolution in the late 1530s.

Follow a wide path uphill through woodlands.

Approach the **Drummer Boy Stone** named after its shape and then alongside a sports field to a stile. Here is the first and very impressive view of Easby Abbey.

The route eases its way around the abbey which should be explored.

Drive and Stroll

Run by English Heritage the ruins are open daily from 11 am to 6 pm and admission is free. There is also a small free car park. The abbey was founded in 1152 with funds provided by Radald who was an influential Norman and the constable of Richmond Castle. He gave the land to the abbey 'for the good of his soul'. It first belonged to the Premonstratensian order, which was founded by St Norbet of Premontre Laon in France. Later their abbeys were taken over by the Cistercians. Although known as the White Monks they were actually canons, which meant that they were also priests and therefore had more contact with the people.

Richmond Falls

The nearby parish church of St Agatha is even older than the abbey and parts of it date to Saxon times but with a substantial rebuild in the early Norman period. In 1994 English Heritage restored the wall paintings dating from around 1250. These need to be protected but can be viewed by a means of a coin-operated light switch.

 6

From the church approach the car park and turn right. This leads along a wide track through extensive **Abbey Wood** overlooked by the fast moving waters of the River Swale.

 7

Approach a substantial railway

bridge. The now disused track was built in 1846 to link Richmond with Darlington. It closed in 1970 since which time it has been part of a footpath linking the town with the abbey. Cross the bridge and follow the old track back to **Richmond**.

The stationmaster's house is now a private residence. The station buildings house a swimming pool and leisure centre, the Arriva bus service area and a garden retail establishment. There is also a substantial free car park set among attractive cottages overlooking the Swale.

 8

At the station turn left up along the main road. Pass the parish church on the right and a school on the left. Climb a steep incline and then turn left into the market square and the starting point.

12 Nun Monkton

The village pond at Nun Monkton

The Walk 1½ miles ⏱ 1½ hours
Map OS Landranger 105 (GR 509578)

How to get there

The village is situated in a cul-de-sac signed off the A59 linking Harrogate with York. Less than 10 miles from the busy city, Nun Monkton is a quiet backwater. **Parking**: There is street parking alongside the large village green.

Drive and Stroll

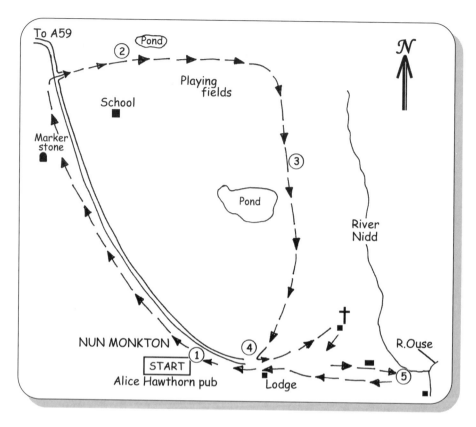

Introduction

Here is an example of an unspoiled village dating back to Saxon times and sited at the confluence of the River Nidd with the Ouse, which then flows on into York. This short stroll, which should on no account be rushed, explores the surroundings of fields, ponds and red-roofed dwellings. The word Nun was added to Monkton at the formation of the Benedictine Priory set up in the 12th century. This is close to the two rivers and these joys are reached along permissive footpaths. The rural tranquillity is enhanced by horses being exercised along wide bridle paths.

The Alice Hawthorn

The 'horse theme' is reflected in the name of the village hostelry which, until 1900, was known as the Blue Bell. The name was changed to celebrate a local racehorse of the 1840s. The mare won her first race in 1841 and went on to win 50.5 races from 69 starts. The 0.5 relates to a dead heat in the days when electronic finishes could not be recorded. Alice Hawthorn was retired to stud and produced Thornaby which won the Derby in 1860. If this horse was impressive then so is the menu at lunchtime and in the evening. The lamb in port wine, the home-made steak pie and the sausage and mash are mouth-watering. The wine list is small but impressive, the Yorkshire beers well represented and the hostelry prides itself on its wide selection of coffees.

The interior walls are enhanced by a collection of Second World War photographs of aircraft and servicemen, a reminder of the days when Canadian aircrew were based at the Bomber Command airfield at nearby Linton-on-Ouse. Telephone: 01423 330303.

THE WALK

(1)

From the **Alice Hawthorn** turn left onto the track through the village, following the very minor narrow road and a cul-de-sac.

Look out to the left for an inscribed stone which should be regarded as the focal point of the village. This dates back to Saxon times and was important enough to be mentioned in the Domesday Book. At this time it was known as Monechetone. This area has not been much altered since Saxon times, but away to the right is the school and red-roofed houses which have replaced the Saxon thatched dwellings.

Continue along the road through the village.

  (2)

As the road leads off towards the A59 turn sharp right along a wide track. Pass the school on the right. There is a pond and houses to the left and playing fields to the right. Away to the left towards the A59 the equestrian theme is maintained because here is the York Harness Racing Track. During meetings Nun Monkton becomes vibrant but on most days it is just an idyllic haven of tranquillity.

  (3)

Turn right across the playing fields and follow the wide track between the houses and the large village pond.

This is a haven for wildfowl especially in the winter. It also provides drinking water for cattle which have been present since Saxon times. The 18-acre green is still used freely by the locals who retain the grazing rights on the common. The cattle and the local folk share the pond. Families often gather to feed bread to the locally-owned geese and the wild birds. Mallards and moorhens are always present but in the winter they are joined by tufted duck and pochard.

Continue along the green and approach a cattle grid and a metal stile and gate.

 4

Pass through the gate and reach the **Priory Lodge**. Turn left. Continue along a pretty avenue of trees and then through another metal gate. This leads to the parish church of **St Mary's**, which was formerly the religious focus of the Benedictine nunnery.

This was built in 1153 and is hailed by experts as one of the best examples of Norman architecture to be found in England. Pass through the archway and if you have time, enter the peace of the church, which is open during daylight hours.

It seems that until Henry VIII dissolved all such institutions in 1536 the nuns led a quiet life except for one incident in 1397. The ladies were then under the guidance of Prioress Margaret Fairfax but became 'associated' with males, adorned themselves with jewellery and even dipped their fingers into the coffers.

It is, however, best to remember the peace of this wonderful building before exploring the equally, if

contrastingly, beautiful stretch of river.

Return to the Priory Gate and turn left. Pass the complex of privately-owned Priory Hall buildings. Look for a clearly marked signpost to the left. This is a permissive path leading through a grassy track. Here is the confluence of the **River Nidd** away to the left with the Ouse straight ahead.

Boats are still in evidence here, a reminder of the time when rowboat ferries operated at the confluence and at nearby Beningbrough on

Nun Monkton church

The River Ouse with the Nidd on the left

the Nidd. In modern times we take fast roads and bridges over rivers for granted. In the Middle Ages until the 19th century, however, river crossings were vital. Rowboat ferries were busy and the fees of travellers usually went into the coffers of religious houses until the dissolution. Private enterprises prospered but it was usual for a fee to be paid to the Crown.

From the river 'crossing' retrace your steps along the footpath. Turn right and then left. After the Priory Lodge pass through the metal gate. Turn left to the **Alice Hawthorn pub**.

13 Long Marston and Marston Moor

The obelisk on Marston Moor

The Walk 7 miles ⏱ 3 hours
Map OS Landranger 105 (GR 502512)

How to get there

Less than 10 miles from York along the A59 towards Harrogate is Long Marston. Pass through Upper Poppleton and then look for a minor road signed Long Marston and Tockwith. At a junction, turn left and follow the road into Long Marston. At the Sun Inn, cross the B1224 into the village. **Parking**: There is no designated parking except at the Sun but Long Marston is seldom busy and there is plenty of parking alongside the green.

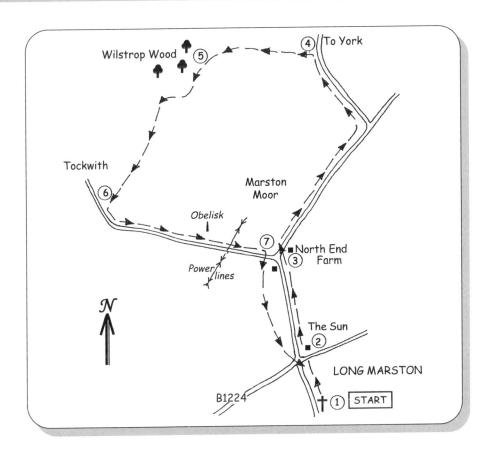

Introduction

This stroll leads from Long Marston along a network of quiet roads, bridleways and footpaths and close to the equally impressive village of Tockwith. The route skirts around Marston Moor, the site of one of the most important battles of the Civil War. The site was rural then and this is still the case. There can be few battlefield walks where most of the important landmarks can still clearly be seen. Here is also the place to inspire naturalists with hedgerow flowers in summer and flocks of migrating birds to be seen during the cooler months of the year.

The Sun Inn

Some time should be spent in exploring the exterior of this one-time coaching inn. It was originally set astride a network of packhorse routes and drove roads which suggests that it was an important hostelry at the time of the battle of Marston Moor. Cromwell and Prince Rupert no doubt knew of it but neither would have had the leisure to enjoy its solid vernacular architecture.

Surprisingly Long Marston is not on the tourist map and so the Sun has to satisfy the local people with regard to its menu. Here, therefore, are substantial meals, including soups to set the mouth watering, steak and ham with a local flavour, good beer and also a surprisingly good brew of tea. Telephone: 01904 738258.

THE WALK

Start the walk at All Saints church. There is a notice indicating where the key can be obtained. It is worth the effort because here are Norman features and evidence of an even earlier foundation. The Norman doorway set in a brickwork construction whilst not unique is certainly unusual and very attractive. The quiet solitude of the churchyard is an ideal preparation for this walk which concerns itself with one of the bloodiest battles in English history.

From the church gate turn right and descend into the village. Pass the village green to the left and then approach the B1224.

At the **Sun Inn** cross the road and continue straight ahead passing attractive residences on each side. These date from the 17th century to the present day but the village has certainly not yet been dominated by modern developments.

Look out for North End Farm set at a T-junction of minor roads. Turn right and continue for some distance along a quiet road. Keep looking left to see the open countryside over which the battle of Marston Moor was fought. At a junction turn left at a sign indicating York (8 miles).

4

Look out for a bridle path sign which indicates that **Tockwith** is 5 kms to the left. Take this path.

It is strange how we in Britain cannot quite make up our minds. Some signs are in miles and some in kilometres. I suppose the Saxons had the same problem. Did they speak old Anglo-Saxon or Norman French?

Here is a stretch of idyllic English countryside. The woodlands in 1644 provided cover for troops and their essential ordnance whilst the open areas allowed the opposing armies to line up and deploy in good order.

The Sun Inn, Long Marston

  (5)

At **Wilstrop Wood** the route sweeps to the left.

This wood provides joy to botanists with plants such as hedge woundwort, betony, self-heal and meadowsweet all having medicinal uses especially in the treatment of wounds. When we think of battles we only think of the dead – but who treated the injured? There is evidence to show that skilled herbalists were present on the battlefields of old England. Bird life is also present here in the woods with tawny owl, jay, woodpigeon and sparrowhawks breeding in some numbers.

Continue along this delightful track to meet a minor road.

  (6)

To the right is the village of Tockwith which is slightly larger than Long Marston. Our route, however, turns left and leads to an obelisk.

The obelisk demands a long stop. It commemorates the battle of Marston Moor fought between the

Roundheads led by Cromwell himself and the Cavaliers under the command of Prince Rupert.

On 2nd July 1644 Cromwell gained a vital victory but not without substantial casualties on both sides. Some 34,000 men and 14,000 horses charged into each other across an open landscape. This aspect can be seen by looking out from the obelisk today even after the Enclosure Acts of the 18th century reduced the size of the fields. The number killed is not known with any certainty but estimates vary from 4,150 to 7,000. Some Royalist survivors fled to York guided there by a beacon's flame lit each night on the tower of the church of All Saints Pavement in York.

Many of the dead were buried on the battlefield itself but some of the injured may have been tended at and around the churches of Long Marston and Tockwith.

From the obelisk, cross under the huge power lines and alongside the minor road. This is actually more like a footpath because the grassy roadside verges are very wide and worth exploring. The variety of flowers is fascinating and includes white deadnettle, betony and bittersweet.

Look out for a footpath pointing right and follow this back to the **Sun Inn** and beyond this to the village of **Long Marston**.

14 Wass and Byland Abbey

Byland Abbey

The Walk 5½ miles ⏱ 3 hours
Map OS Landranger 100 (GR 548791)

How to get there

Take the A170 from Thirsk to Helmsley. Turn off right on a minor road to Wass. Byland Abbey is signed from Wass. Do not confuse Byland Abbey with Old Byland which is some distance to the north and close to Rievaulx Abbey. **Parking**: There is street parking around Byland Abbey and in Wass.

Drive and Stroll

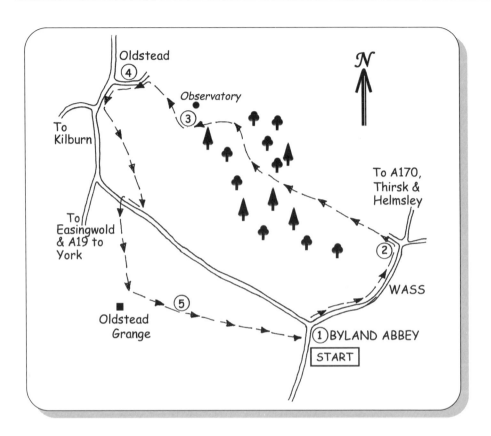

Introduction

This stroll should persuade all to follow the road and 'lift their eyes to the heavens'. Where else is it possible to enjoy the splendid ruins of a Cistercian abbey close to which a Victorian astronomical observatory stands high on a hill? Those who worship the natural world will not be disappointed either and throughout the undulating stroll there are panoramic views of Yorkshire scenery at its best.

The Abbey Inn

This inn has a wonderful history and its three en-suite rooms are locally famous and the quality and atmosphere of the place is remarkable.

The Cistercian monks were renowned for their hospitality and may well have entertained guests on the present site. In 1322 King Edward II was being entertained at Byland when the Scots under Robert the Bruce attacked the area. The monastic inn was closed when Henry VIII dissolved the abbey in 1537 but around 1845 a group of Benedictines from nearby Ampleforth re-established the Abbey Inn. Since 1997 it has been privately owned. It has been refurbished and is run with great attention to detail. The food is to say the least imaginative. Telephone: 01347 868204.

THE WALK

Start at Byland Abbey, the ruins of which are administered by English Heritage. It is closed in winter but the views of the substantial ruins are magnificent when seen from the roadside.

In 1134 a group of Savigniac monks (later the Cistercians) set off from Furness Abbey, now in Cumbria, and founded a daughter house. After several unsuccessful moves they finally settled permanently at Byland in 1177. At its most prosperous in the 14th century Byland was said to be the largest ecclesiastical building in Europe. When Henry VIII dissolved the abbeys Byland was 'slighted' but what is left of its mighty church and splendid Rose Window is still impressive. The tiled floors have also survived surprisingly well. These are said to be the finest examples in the whole of Europe.

 ①

From the abbey bear right along a well-marked public footpath. Then follow a right turn and pass between gates. After another series of gates a road is reached.

 ②

To the right is the little village of **Wass** which is well worth exploring. Our walk, though, leads left to a sign marked Observatory. A steep climb through a woodland leads to a stile. Turn left and then turn right (there are two other minor paths to the left but be sure to ignore these). Continue to climb until an open space is reached and provides time to draw breath. Take a left towards **Oldstead Observatory**.

Oldstead Observatory was set up by John Wormald of Oldstead Hall in 1838. He dedicated his sky watches to the accession to the throne of Queen Victoria. Set on a hill at an elevation of 1,146 feet (340 metres) the observatory building itself is impressive and is 40 feet (12 metres) high. In those days the distant views from the roof-mounted telescope would not have been obscured by any form of industrial smoke.

 ③

Keep the observatory to the right and descend a steep path. Turn right at a sign indicating Oldstead. This reaches a lane.

The rear of the Abbey Inn

 (4)

Approach a T-junction and turn left. Pass through a set of gateposts and over a cattle grid. Continue along a field path to a minor road. Turn sharp right and after a short distance turn left and follow an obvious path. Pass to the left of **Oldstead Grange**. The monks set up the Grange (farm) and they also had extensive fishponds on the site.

 (5)

Byland Abbey is well signed from this point and as the track leads through fields and over stiles look for depressions in the ground.

These mark the position of other extensive fishponds developed by the monks. The brethren ate a lot of fish and even had methods of making carp taste reasonable. They did eat meat but this was often in short supply. They grew corn and vegetables and, although experts in water management, they also enjoyed their wine and ale. They also kept bees as sugar was not known in the Middle Ages and honey was the accepted sweetner.

Pass through a wooded area to a minor road. Turn left and return to the abbey.

15 Hutton-le-Hole

Hutton-le-Hole

The Walk 5 miles 🕐 2½ hours
Map OS Landranger 100 (GR 705899)

How to get there

Hutton-le-Hole is situated 7 miles north-west of Pickering. Travelling west from Pickering on the A170 turn right near Kirkbymoorside on a minor road to Hutton-le-Hole. **Parking**: There is parking in the village.

Drive and Stroll

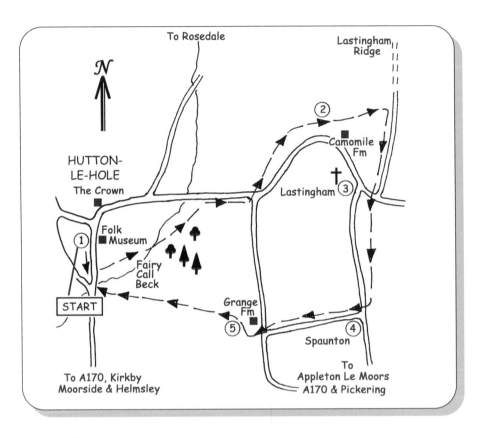

Introduction

This stroll has a distinctly religious feel to it. There was a Christian monastery at Lastingham in the 7th century, and, in the more austere 17th century, Hutton-le-Hole was a safe refuge for Quakers. As such Hutton-le-Hole is a mecca for Americans because of its association with William Penn who helped found Pennsylvania. The Ryedale Folk Museum traces the history of the village and the region back some 400 years, whilst naturalists delight in Westfield Wood which enfolds Hutton, listed as Hoton in the Domesday survey, and through which a series of streams flows down from the surrounding hills.

The Crown Hotel

This is an excellent place to build up strength before a walk or to recover after your exertions. It does not offer accommodation but the beer selection, the lunch and dinner menu are comprehensive and many people drop in for tea or coffee. The restaurant, however, is closed on Tuesdays. Local meat features strongly on the menu and the vegetarian choice is wide. The fisherman's pie can be recommended. The beamed ceilings have hundreds of decorated jugs hanging from hooks, adding a unique character to the hostelry, as does the welcoming log fire. Telephone: 01751 417343.

THE WALK

Start at the **Ryedale Folk Museum**, which is open from Easter to the end of October.

The open-air complex consists of buildings set in 2.5 acres (1 hectare). Still in a fascinating state of development, here are thatched cottages, farms and an Elizabethan manor house all brought to the museum and assembled on site. Here, too, is the oldest photographic studio remaining in Britain, which dates back to 1849. The museum is rightly celebrating being given a Heritage Lottery Grant, the results of which will become apparent from 2005 onwards. On the opposite side of the Crown look out for John Richardson's Quaker College dating to 1695. John spent time in America with William Penn before returning to his home village, which he chose as his last resting place.

From the Beckside gift shop turn left at a marked track at the **Barn Hotel**. Follow the track first over stiles and then across a footbridge over the delightfully named **Fairy Call Beck**. Pass through woodland and turn right along a minor road and then left into a series of fields.

The track here is well signed and descends into a tree-lined valley. Cross a tiny stream over a stile and through a kissing gate. **Camomile Farm** is to the right before meeting the **Lastingham Ridge** track. Continue on into **Lastingham**.

Lastingham is one of the most important Christian sites in Britain and St Cedd founded a monastery here in AD 654. The bulk of this monastery has obviously gone but in the year 2000 a Millennium boulder was inscribed with a cross and set on a hillside above the village.

The church of St Mary is open during daylight hours which is a real bonus on this walk. Steps from the chancel lead down into the Norman crypt dating to 1078 and here is the resting place of St Cedd who died at Lastingham after attending the Synod at Whitby in 664 AD. This meeting resulted in agreement between the Celtic and Roman Catholic churches.

🐾 ③

At Lastingham Green find an obvious sign indicating Copton, Pickering and Rosedale. Follow this sign and then turn right over a little bridge. Climb towards a footpath sign and continue to ascend through woods to a gate.

The Norman crypt at Lastingham church

🐾 ④

Turn right to **Spaunton**.

Here is an attractive hamlet with its street lined with cottages and farms many dating to the 17th century. The fields surrounding the settlement are still set out in the Roman pattern and a burial ground of this period has been found close by. In the 1940s the foundations of a medieval hall were discovered, proving that Spaunton was once a large settlement, probably administered by St Mary's Abbey in York. In the 1530s Henry VIII dissolved the abbey and all its lands were sold. At Spaunton the new owners set up a Court Leet with one of the guarantees giving local people the right to graze stock on common land (see walk no. 13 at Nun Monkton).

From Spaunton turn right along a minor road. At a T-junction follow a footpath straight ahead passing **Grange Farm** to the right.

🐾 ⑤

Follow the path down into a woodland area. As the path divides take the left fork. Descend towards **Fairy Call Beck** and look for a stile. This leads to a road. Turn right and return to **Hutton-le-Hole**.

The village is dissected by a tumbling stream and its green on either side is one of the most attractive in the North.

16 Wharram Percy, near Malton

The Walk 2½ miles ⏱ 1½ hours
Map OS Explorer 300 (GR 855645)

How to get there

From Malton travel south-east to take the B1248 through Norton and North Grimston. Pass through Wharram-le-Street and turn right for Wharram Percy Medieval Village, indicated by an English Heritage brown sign. **Parking**: The substantial track leads to a free car park on the right after about ½ mile.

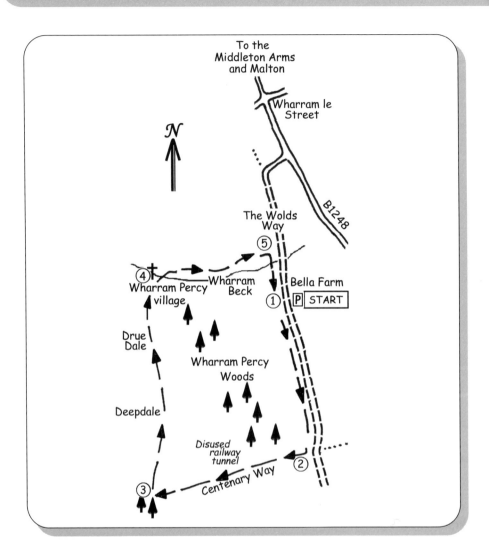

Introduction

Wharram Percy is acknowledged as the best-preserved deserted village in Europe. The place is hauntingly beautiful and this stroll around the village offers a feeling of splendid isolation. On the way there are crystal clear springs, undulating footpaths and wildlife combining to enchant walkers of all ages. Roe deer and jay are regularly sighted whilst it is also possible to spot the red kite, which has very recently been reintroduced into the area.

All this means that this walk has everything the historian or the naturalist could hope for except for modern developments. What a joy!

The Middleton Arms

Obviously there is no hostelry in a deserted village and so my recommended stop is the Middleton Arms at North Grimston. This is a particularly relevant place to visit because, in 1833, Henry Lord Middleton bought the land hereabouts, including Wharram Percy. The family still own the site but allow English Heritage to manage it.

The Middleton Arms looks just what it once was – a substantial 18th-century farmhouse which later became an inn. There is a warm welcome inside, with morning coffee, snacks and lunches served daily, whilst the impressive dinner menu is on offer every evening from 7 pm to 9 pm. Local produce is always on the menu and there is a wide choice of ales. At the rear is an extensive beer garden and a play area for children. There is also plenty of space to park. Telephone: 01944 768255.

THE WALK

Before setting off, take time to explore the area near the English Heritage car park at Wharram Percy and to read the notice boards depicting the history of the place.

From the car park, do not descend the track but go uphill for a few yards and turn immediately right along a substantial bridleway. This is **Centenary Way** – a new route to celebrate the year 2000. Follow this track, passing a large woodland on the right dominated by conifers. Pause close to the woodland and look to the right.

Beneath the route is the old Burdale railway tunnel completed in 1853 to link Driffield and Malton. This ill-fated structure leaked from the beginning and the line itself was very short-lived. Still visible, however, are a number of old airshafts bored and chimneyed to ventilate the tunnel. At point 4 of the walk, you can see a few blocks of stone, all that is left of a pump house built in an attempt to remove water from the tunnel.

Continue to follow the Centenary Way, which is clearly marked by yellow arrows.

Turn sharp right into **Deepdale**. This is indeed a deep valley and the route is obvious but care must be taken in wet weather when good boots or wellingtons are essential. Continue to follow the yellow arrows along Deepdale and as the village of

Wharram Percy is approached Deepdale joins **Drue Dale**.

Both Deepdale and Drue Dale are full of little springs and streams which keep disappearing underground. This is because the valley bottom is composed of a mixture of chalk and clay. The chalk is porous and soaks up the water whilst the clay holds it and allows it to emerge again on the surface. This reliable water supply explains why there was a settlement hereabouts as far back as Celtic times. Drue Dale could, in fact, be a corruption of Druids Dale but not all historians agree with this interpretation. I ask the question, though: if this isn't the case then how else did the place get its name?

Pass through a kissing gate and enter the village.

There is a pond to the right whose water supply is controlled by sluices and in the 9th century, two corn mills operated from here. Although these mills were abandoned in the 12th century the monks of Haltemprice Priory, near Hull, used this place as a fishery.

From the pond follow the obvious track to **St Martin's** churchyard and cemetery.

Remains dating from the Stone, Bronze, and Iron ages, as well as from the Roman and Anglo-Saxon period have been found here. St Martin's itself dates from the 10th century but the building we see today and which was once a substantial parish church dates mainly to the 14th century. There are some splendid arcades and although damaged by weather and the ravages of time, St Martin's is still an atmospheric building. Part of the tower collapsed in 1959 and the roof was removed for safety reasons.

Before you leave the village, take time to explore the humps and bumps and read the weatherproof information boards, which English Heritage has produced. By the 15th century the village was in decline partly because of the effects of the *Black Death but also because the local population began to make their living from the wool trade which was far less labour-intensive than mixed agricultural farming.*

Take an obvious track (the only one) that leads down out of the village. The track descends to **Wharram Beck** and at this point the walk also follows the long distance footpath called the **Wolds Way**.

The reason that Wharram Beck runs is because of its clay bed and this is also why the stroll can be sticky in wet weather.

 (5)

Cross the beck which passes close to the old Malton railway line. Ascend a few steps and take the obvious track which climbs steeply for around ½ mile and passes through three kissing gates. Pass fields and **Bella Farm** to the left and ascend to the car park.

17 | Goathland

The super hostelry at Goathland

The Walk 5 miles ⏱ 2½ hours
Map OS Landranger 94 (GR 838024)

How to get there

From Pickering on the A170 turn north on the A169 and continue towards Whitby which is only 7 miles away. A left turn along a minor road leads to Goathland. **Parking**: There is parking in the village and a pay and display area at the railway.

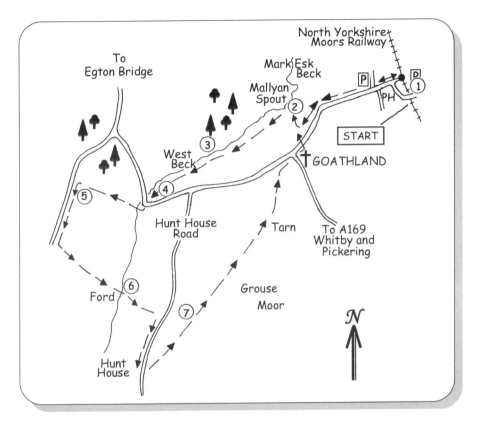

Introduction

Goathland is now famous as the location for the fictitious village of Aidensfield in the epic TV series *Heartbeat*. The village is on the North Yorkshire railway route. The Whitby to Pickering railway opened on 26th May 1836 and was engineered by George Stephenson, with the intention of using horses as the motive power. It closed during the Beeching cuts of the 1960s but the tourist railway was opened on 1st May 1973. At almost 20 miles, it is the second longest in Britain.

The walk follows rippling streams over fields and up onto moorlands with the added bonus of tumbling waterfalls. The route also passes close to an impressive stretch of the Wheeldale Roman road known as Wade's Way. Goathland is one of the few English villages which celebrates Plough Monday which takes place on the first Monday after 6th January. In the old days it was celebrated as a farm worker's holiday. The plough is paraded through the streets to the church where it is blessed.

Drive and Stroll

The Mallyan Spout Hotel

This is a fine hostelry with good accommodation on offer in and around the old stable block. The Victorians were great travellers and the inn proved popular. This is still the case as the dinner menu is most impressive and varied. Lunch times are popular as the Spout welcomes walkers. The choice of cheeses, both local and international, is worth a journey on its own and local grouse and pheasant are often on the menu and should not be missed. Telephone: 0870 701 4444.

THE WALK

Start at the pay and display railway car park. Ascend a hill and turn right through the village.

The huge village green dates back many centuries and is surrounded by pretty red-roofed cottages. Find the church of St Mary on the left which only dates to around 1890 but is attractive for all that. Opposite the church pass through a gate near to the Mallyan Spout Hotel. Look beyond the hotel to the stretch of Roman road.

Follow a signed path to **Mallyan Spout**.

This is one of a series of waterfalls in the area. Mallyan tumbles 70 feet (21 metres) and at times of rain West Beck can be very impressive. Care needs to be taken as the approach is steep and can be very slippery after rain or frost. The spray from the spout provides the perfect habitat for several species of fern and moss which attract academic botanists.

The slippery path from the spout bears left.

Follow the well marked signs and pass over two footbridges and alongside **Scar Wood** set on the slopes of steep cliffs. Keep **West Beck** on the right.

Here is a breeding habitat for dipper and grey wagtail along the riverside, and great spotted and green woodpeckers can be sighted among the trees.

Meet a minor road and turn left for a short distance and then sharp right following a marked bridleway. Cross a bridge and then past a group of buildings. Go over a field, pass through a gate and bear slightly right through woodland. At a gate leading to a narrow road turn left.

Follow a prominent sign indicating

A busy day at Goathland station

the Roman road and continue along a well-used bridleway. Turn left and continue to a ford.

 (6)

Pass over the ford and follow the obvious track and continue between farm buildings before turning left and ascending along a green track. On reaching a minor road turn right. Follow **Hunt House Road** and at Hunt House find a footpath clearly indicated left.

 (7)

Turn left and look out for red grouse all around a moorland area.

The call of this bird is very descriptive because it sounds just like a high pitched and guttural 'Go back, go back'. Their diet consists mainly of the young shoots of heather. This heather looks attractive but in the autumn the moorland turns deep purple. The moorland needs to be managed by means of a burning regime which keeps both the heather young and healthy whilst the bracken growth is prevented.

Pass a small tarn on the right and follow a path indicated by a series of cairns. Finally ease away to the left and descend to a little stream. Pick up a bridleway and descend to the church and through the village and return along the steep road to the station.

18 Staithes

Staithes

The Walk 4 miles 🕒 2½ hours
Map OS Landranger 94 (GR 782185)

How to get there

Situated to the north of Whitby, Staithes is reached from the resort by turning right off the A174. **Parking**: There is a good pay and display car park above the village and there is then a steep stroll down to the harbour. Disabled visitors can drive down to the harbour.

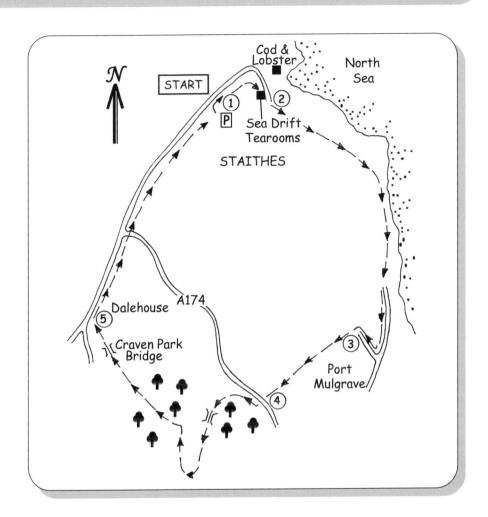

Introduction

Sandwiched between the headlands of Cowbar Nab and Penny Nab, Staithes is a maze of cobbled streets running up steeply from the harbour. Today, it looks to be a rival to the coastal villages of Devon and Cornwall but this belies its industrial past This stroll passes Port Mulgrave which was a purpose-built harbour designed to export ironstone. Looking out to sea, it is easy to imagine why the young James Cook decided in 1741 to give up his job as a grocer's assistant in Staithes and sign on as a cabin boy in Whitby. The rest, as they say, is history.

Drive and Stroll

The Cod & Lobster and the Sea Drift Café

A look at the tiny pub named the Cod and Lobster shows how the sea pounding into the harbour has resulted in several reconstructions. Although no food is available, the beer is always excellent and picnic tables are provided overlooking the harbour.

Close to the Cod & Lobster is the Sea Drift Café, famous for the variety of its sandwiches and home-made cakes but especially for the quality of its coffees. The tea is also excellent and can be enjoyed inside or outside on benches overlooking the little harbour hemmed in by towering sea cliffs, the haunt of sea birds all the year round.

THE WALK

From the car park turn right and descend the steep path down to the harbour. Pass the **Cod & Lobster** and turn right and ascend a steep road.

Clustered around the harbour and along the steep banks of the Roxby Beck are attractive cottages and narrow streets. Look for the Captain Cook Heritage Centre and the brightly-coloured boats called cobles tied up on the beach. These vessels are described as clinker-built which means that they are constructed to a Viking design with the planks overlapping downwards. The cobles were also designed to be launched directly from the beach.

Continue uphill and bear left up a narrow gulley. Follow the path, which winds uphill and onto the cliff edge. This leads to a narrow road.

Turn right and then left to **Port Mulgrave**.

Continue into Port Mulgrave.

The dilapidated appearance of the place belies the fact that it was once a busy port. Look out for a long tunnel near the foot of the cliffs because for nearly a century until it closed in 1920 a railway track led inland for a mile to the ironstone mines at Dalehouse to the south of Staithes. Iron ore was carried by narrow gauge railway and tipped directly into the holds of waiting coasters. It was then sent to the iron furnaces including a number around Jarrow. Decay then set in but the demise of the port was completed by demolition teams at the onset of the Second World War. They had to ensure that the invading Germans could not make use of the harbour.

At the village turn right and then take an obvious left turn across fields.

The tiny pub on the harbour in Staithes

  (4)

Cross the A174 and bear right into woodland and then left. Cross a footbridge over a small stream. Bear left and ascend a track. This swings back on itself and into another woodland area. Carry on, past the Caravan Park Bridge to **Dalehouse**.

 (5)

At Dalehouse, where the ironstone mines were once located, turn right along the road. At a road junction carry straight on and return to the car park in **Staithes**.

The village has not entirely lost its industrial heritage, because two miles away at Boulby a potash mine was opened as late as 1972. There is, however, lots of ancient history and it is thought that Beowulf, a 6th-century Viking, may have been buried here facing the sea on Boulby cliff, which at 655 feet (202 metres) is the highest point on the North Yorkshire coast. The walk around Staithes should be regarded both literally and metaphorically as a high point of any Yorkshire stroll.

19 Robin Hood's Bay

Down at the waters' edge. In the background is the Lifeboat Museum

The Walk 2½ miles ⏱ 2 hours
Map OS Landranger 94 (GR 951055)

How to get there

Robin Hood's Bay is situated off the A171 road between Whitby and Scarborough. At High Hawsker, turn off along the B1447 which leads to the village. **Parking**: There is a pay and display car park on the site of the old railway station. In the winter the car park is free.

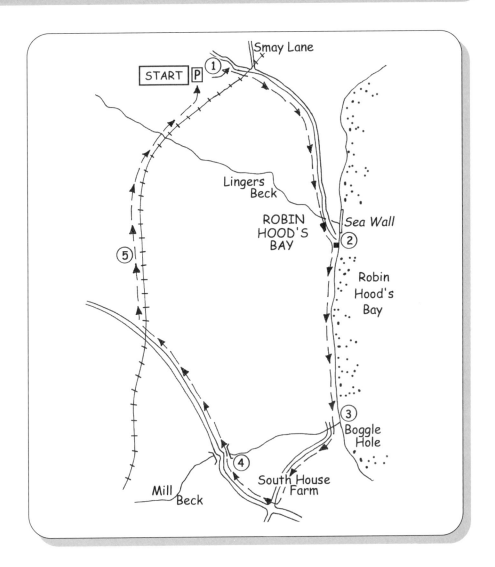

Introduction

From this spectacular walk, the views to seaward are magnificient, with the red pantiled roofs of the cottages clinging to the cliffs, resembling a colony of perched sea birds. This is the haunt of the geologist in search of the fossils contained in the unstable Jurassic strata laid down some 150 million years ago. Part of the stroll follows the coastline and the rock pools are regarded as

Drive and Stroll

some of the finest in Britain. The history and natural history is exciting and the sheer beauty found on this undulating walk is as fine as any to be found in Britain and makes the outing well worth the effort involved.

The Bramblewick Tearooms and Restaurant

Situated 20 yards from the harbour, the building dates to 1646 and was originally three fishermen's cottages. In later times it was a bakery which doubled up as a place where locals could have their Sunday joints cooked in the ovens.

Bramblewick has three impressive en-suite bedrooms and is famous for the quality of its tea and coffee whilst the restaurant is well respected by locals and visitors alike. Walkers are sure of a warm welcome and the breakfasts are substantial and beautifully cooked. Take away sandwiches are prepared to order, not only for those staying overnight but for all visitors. Telephone: 01947 880960.

THE WALK

Start at the car park on the site of the old railway station and close to the **Victoria Hotel**.

The 21-mile railway (34 km) ran from Scarborough to Whitby and was opened to traffic in 1885. It closed in 1965 but there are plenty of sections along the old track which can be walked.

From the car park, turn left and then right down the very steep street into the village. Follow the narrow main street with steps on one side and a twisting motor road, **Smay Lane**, on the other. Cross **Lingers Beck** on its way to the sea.

The most accurate name for the settlement is Bay Town because the Robin Hood connection seems to be somewhat tenuous. Legend has it that the Abbot of Whitby employed Robin Hood to rid the area of pirates! Look for cottages dating between 1650 and 1750 when they were occupied by seamen, fishermen and many who earned a less respectable living by smuggling. Here also are cottages once owned by whaling mariners who either lived or retired to Robin Hood's from their Whitby base.

Continue down to the little harbour.

Its strengthened sea wall was completed in 1974, although the sea is still a constant threat. The beach has been the training ground for marine biologists and during the 1960s I myself taught at the laboratory set up by Sheffield

A novel collecting box outside the Lifeboat Museum

University on the site of the old coastguard station. This was established by the Prince Regent in 1822, who later became George IV. It is pleasing to find that the building has now resorted to something relating to its former function. A splendid little lifeboat museum is staffed by volunteers whilst outside a fish with an open mouth begs coins from visitors and helps to defray the costs of the building. All buildings on the harbour, including the Bay Hotel, are constantly battered by the winds and waves.

Take the upper path and turn left up **Albion Road** and follow the signs for the **Cleveland Way**. Continue on to **Boggle Hole**.

Cross **Mill Beck**.

This tumbles its way down to the sea along a course which over the centuries it has ground out of the Boggle Hole rocks. A watermill, once powered by the beck, has functioned as a youth hostel since 1951. For almost three centuries the old mill ground flour and cattle feed, and ships laden with grain were off-loaded at Boggle Hole.

Turn right after the beck and ascend a narrow lane. Pass cottages and turn right at **South House Farm**.

Cross **Mill Beck** via a footbridge and bear right and then left to reach the track of the old railway. Turn right along the old track.

The building of this railway track was not an easy feat of engineering. It involved the construction of two tunnels and a substantial viaduct. The steep inclines meant that even powerful locomotives could not pull trains faster than an average of 20 miles per hour.

Continue along the old track. Cross over **Lingers Beck** and return to the site of the station car park.

20 Ravenscar

The Walk 4 miles ⏱ 2 hours
Map OS Landranger 94 (GR 978018)

How to get there

Follow the A171 from Scarborough towards Whitby. Turn right along a minor road and pass through Cloughton and Staintondale to Ravenscar. This is a seaside resort which never was and is situated at the end of a cul-de-sac. **Parking**: There is street parking close to the Raven Hall Hotel off Station Road. Here also is the National Trust Coastal Exhibition Centre, which is open during the summer.

Drive and Stroll

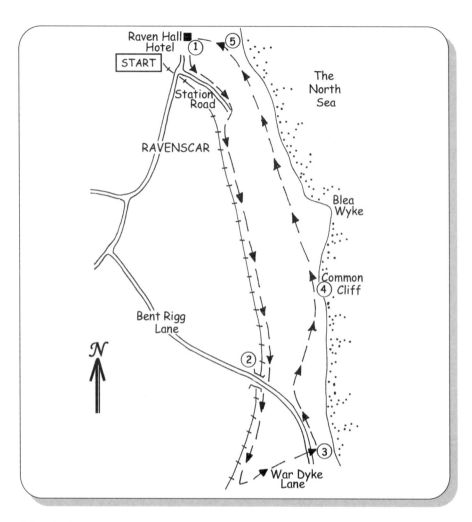

Introduction

The views from the cliffs hereabouts are spectacular and the National Trust has been proactive in publicising the tourist potential of the area. The Ravenscar Coastal Centre includes a history of the 'Town that never was', an explanation of fossils and a marine aquarium. Walking guides and leaflets are available.

It is difficult to imagine what this cliff-top stroll would have been like if Victorian property developers had realised their dream. In the 1890s the Peak Estate Company employed more than 300 men and intended to create an elegant seaside resort. Houses, hotels and shops were planned and free rail trips were run for prospective purchasers based in such towns as Leeds and Bradford.The company hoped to sell up to 1,500 plots but buyers were reluctant. Then along came the First World War. In 1923 the company went bankrupt.

The Raven Hall Hotel

Built by Richard Hammon in 1774 on the site of a Roman signal station, the Raven Hall offers magnificent views over the ruggedly beautiful coastline. Hammon was a friend of George III and before he became insane the monarch spent periods at Raven Hall.

The hotel owned by the same family since 1961 is now in a splendid state of repair and is the focus of a golf course and leisure complex. The views from the terrace are as fine as any in the county. The food offered is second to none, and sandwiches and snacks can be enjoyed on the terraces. Walkers should be aware, however, that dogs are not allowed in the grounds. Telephone: 01723 870353.

THE WALK

Begin close to the **Raven Hall Hotel** and its associated golf course situated on **Station Road**.

This area of Ravenscar is at one end of the Lyke Lake Walk which crosses the North Yorkshire Moors. The village also stands on the 36-mile stretch of coastline known as the North Yorkshire and Cleveland Heritage Coast which runs from Scarborough to Saltburn.

Turn right into **Station Square** and follow the line of the railway, which closed in 1965.

Cross a bridge and continue along the old line. Look left to a stile, descend a set of steps and then ascend along a steep track.

Approach the narrow **War Dyke Lane**. Turn left and then bear right to reach **Common Cliff**.

The route followed here is on solid ground and the views are said to be the best in North Yorkshire. This is the place to enjoy spectacular scenery and exciting bird watching. Look out for breeding fulmars and auks especially guillemots. In winter birds such as shearwaters and divers can be seen over and on the sea, some 600 feet below. The occasional gannet, Britain's largest and most graceful seabird soars above the waves. Here are breeding colonies of razorbills and guillemots

Drive and Stroll

plus those of the kittiwake, whose gentle calls send the phrase kit-ee-wake echoing around the cliffs.

 4

Follow the track from **Common Cliff** to the coastguard lookout station and **Blea Wyke**.

The flowers hereabouts attract

botanists from all over Britain to view them. They include mallow, bindweed, lady's bedstraw and several species of trefoil, plus sweet scented clovers.

 5

As the clifftop path terminates, turn left to reach the Information Centre and the **Raven Hall Hotel**.